CASTLES OF
SCOTLAND

past and present

C. GAMBARO

BARNES & NOBLE BOOKS

NEW YORK

CASTLES OF SCOTLAND
past and present

Texts
Cristina Gambaro

Editing supervision
Giulia Gaida

Graphic design
Patrizia Balocco Lovisetti

Graphic layout
Anna Galliani

Translation by
Neil Frazer Davenport

1 The coat of arms of Mary Stuart at Falkland Palace, one of the royal palaces of the Scottish Stuart dynasty.

2-3 Drummond Castle, with its famous garden, is located in Central Scotland. It stands on a rise and the terraces overlook the marvellous and painstakingly groomed lawns laid in the form of the cross of St Andrew. The sundial in the center dates from 1630.

CONTENTS

© 2005 White Star S.p.a.

This edition published by
Barnes & Noble Publishing, Inc.,
by arrangement with
White Star S.p.a.,
2005 Barnes & Noble Books

M10987654321
ISBN 0-7607-7378-5

Library of Congress
Cataloging-in-Publication
Data available

Color separations by Fotomec, Turin
Printed in China

4 top Eilean Donan Castle, one of the most spectacular in Northern Scotland, takes its name from the island on which it stands. Part of the castle was built in 1220 by Alexander II as a defensive fortress against the Vikings. Later, Alexander III presented it to Colin Fitzgerald, the son of the Irish Earl of Desmond, the ancestor of the McKenzies.

From the establishment of the kingdom of the Scots under King Kenneth MacAlpine in 843 to the Union with the English Crown in 1707, all of the Scottish castles played a principally defensive role. High, turretted and surrounded by walls and bastions they were apparently impregnable and as well as protecting the local lord, served as his administrative center and the residence of his family, servants and soldiers. The fortified tower, or tower house, was the most common form and was found in both the remote Highlands and the fertile valleys of the Borders, at the confine with England. Composed of three storys linked by spiral staircases in stone or wood, the last of which was overhanging, the tower house was a feature of over 1,000 years of Scottish history, from the defensive towers of the Picts and the Scots to the noble palaces of the Victorian era. The form evolved over the centuries with the addition of new elements, but the most fascinating examples are those that have managed to retain the characteristic tower motif. Many have survived such as Threave Castle in Dumfries and Galloway, one of the oldest, and the castles of Craigmillar and Crichton, which were originally two tower houses successively extended. The earliest Scottish fortifications date back to the Iron Age. Between 800 BC and 400 AD there were numerous hill forts, earthworks or stone walls constructed to defend the villages from the neighboring tribes or the incursions of the Romans (AD 71-84). One of the most famous hill forts is located at Dunnadd in Argyll, the ancient capital of the kingdom of Dalriada. Another form of defensive structure were the brochs, tall towers with double walls in stone, cylindrical in form and tapering slightly towards the top. In spite of the Scandinavian origin of their name, the brochs were built long before the arrival of the Norwegians and probably co-existed with the hill forts. They were over thirty-three feet high and were inhabited by the ruling family, but in times of danger they could accommodate up to two hundred persons. Among the best conserved brochs is that of Mousa in the Shetland Islands.

In 1066 the marriage between Malcom III Canmore and Margaret, who

6 top left Caerlaverock Castle has an unusual triangular plan and it conceals an internal facade with symmetrical Renaissance decoration. The principal elements are the semi-circular or triangular windows and the pediment of the doorway sculpted with mythological or heraldic motifs.

6 top right In the 13th century at St. Andrews, on the North coast of the Fife peninsula, a fortified bishop's palace was constructed in which James I and James III were educated. St. Andrews Castle was at the center of the conflict during the religious wars and was almost completely demolished to provide material for the construction of the port's sea-wall.

6-7 and 7 top right The aerial view shows Crathes Castle and its beautiful gardens. Yew hedges separate the Color Garden in which the dominant colors are yellow, red and violet, from the more formal Fountain Garden, based on blue, and the Rose Garden. The most recent creation is the Golden Garden dedicated to the memory of Lady Burnett who was responsible, together with her husband Sir James, for this green oasis.

was raised at court in London, brought Norman customs and traditions to the wild Scotland. The first feudal castles date from this period. The earliest examples took the form of mounds dominated by a wooden tower and surrounded by a moat, at the foot of which stood wooden houses within a courtyard surrounded by a palisade. There are no surviving examples of this "motte-and-bailey" castle, but they are clearly depicted in the Bayeux Tapestry. At Hawick in the Borders, however, the earth mound on which the wooden tower once stood can still be seen. Over the course of the following two centuries stone castles almost completely replaced the old wooden structures. In a number of the castles constructed after the mid-fourteenth century there was an evident desire to improve the defensive capabilities that previously relied exclusively on the buildings' massive structure. In the castle of St. Andrews in Fife, for example, the tower is no longer set in the middle of the bailey and the principal entrance to the castle is incorporated within it. At the end of the fifteenth century decorative and ornamental elements began to increase in importance, especially in the royal residences. The richness of these constructions drew heavily on French Renaissance motifs, probably due to the alliances and close ties of kinship between the Stuarts and the French royal family in that period. Falkland Palace, James V's favorite residence, has nothing in common with

the original tower house, embellished as it is with a wealth of towers, turrets, medallions and pilasters. The sculptural decoration of the North Wall of Crichton Castle in the Borders region, completed in 1585, was moving in the same direction, as was Caerlaverock Castle in Dumfries, in which the massive, austere exterior contrasts with the elegance of the internal courtyard.

This greater attention to the external appearance of the buildings led to the

8 top left Aerial view of Culzean Castle on the West Coast, a few miles from the city of Ayr. Standing on the cliff-top, this is one of the most impressive stately homes in the whole of Scotland, the fruit of the creative genius of Robert Adam who designed it in the 18th century to replace the existing 200-year-old castle.

development of the ornamental potential of the defensive elements. This tendency can be seen in the castles built in the Northeast of Scotland from the late sixteenth century. Castles such as those of Crathes and Fyvie are at the same time both fortresses and elaborate works of art. With the Act of Union of 1707 the Scottish castles' defensive function was made largely redundant. Although for 40 years, up to the massacre of Culloden, the Jacobites maintained their opposition to the Crown, Scotland enjoyed a period of peace. The families of the old nobility, made even richer by the expropriation of terrain from the small landowners, began to build great palaces. They were then flanked by the families of the great merchants and those of the early industrialists who commissioned leading architects to build their homes. The years between the eighteenth and the nineteenth centuries saw the establishment of a successful architectural dynasty, the Adams, sensitive to neo-classical and Italian influences. Among the Adam family's most important creations were the beautiful Charlotte Square in Edinburgh, which in those years was taking on a new elegant and sophisticated appearance, and Hopetoun, Mellerstain and Culzean Castle, characterized by extremely simple, clean external lines contrasting with the opulence of the interiors. In the second half of the last century, thanks to the novels of Sir Walter Scott, Romanticism led to a revival of interest in the Medieval world and the Scottish traditions. Architecture was not immune to this new trend and the period saw the construction of houses decorated with towers, ogives and dark inlaid wood. Sir Walter Scott's own residence, Abbotsford, and Dalmeny House are good examples, while Balmoral Castle, the royal family's summer residence, remains the best example of the neo-baronial style, the leading exponents of which were the architects David Bryce and Gillespie Graham.

Mellerstain House

Scone Palace

Drum Castle

12-13
Castle Tioram, the
powerful castle
belonging to the
MacDonalds of
Clanranald was
built early in the
14th century on a
remote island in
Loch Moidart.
Accessible by land
only at low tide, it
was frequently
attacked by the rival
Campbell clan and
was burned down in
1715.

14-15 The impressive
library of Dunrobin
Castle built by Sir
Robert Lorimer,
contains over ten
thousand volumes,
with numerous rare
and precious editions.
Most of the works are
concerned with the
development of the
Highlands and
Scottish law.
There is also a fine
Chippendale desk and
a 19th-century globe.
A portrait of the
Duchess Eileen Butler
who married the Duke
of Sutherland in 1912
hangs on the wall.
There is a precious
oriental carpet on
the floor.

Thirlestane Castle

Caerlaverock Castle

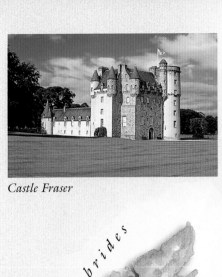
Castle Fraser

Atlantic
Ocean

Orkney
Islands

North
Sea

Outer Hebrides

Thurso

Dunrobin Castle

Oykel

The
Highlands

Inverness

Brodie Castle
Cawdor Castle

Fyvie Castle

Spey

Deveron

Haddo House

Dunvegan
Castle

Don

Castle
Fraser

Drum Castle

Isle
of Skye

Loch Ness

Craigievar Castle

Crathes Castle

Aberdeen

Grampian Mountains

Balmoral

Braemar

Dunnottar Castle

Caledonian Canal

Fort
William

Blair Castle

Loch
Linnhe

Tay

Glamis Castle

Castle
Stalker

Scone Palace

Dundee

Perth

St. Andrews

Mull

Oban

Drummond Castle

Inveraray Castle

Falkland Palace

Hopetoun
House

Loch Lomond

Stirling Castle

Edinburgh

Linlithgow
Palace

Edinburgh Castle
Holyrood

Thirlestane Castle

Glasgow

Mellerstain House

Tweed

Traquair House

Floors Castle

Brodick
Castle

Abbotsford House

Teviot

Arran

Ayr

Culzean Castle

Drumlanrig Castle

Esk

Atlantic
Ocean

Dee

Dumfries

Caerlaverock
Castle

North Channel

Northern
Ireland

England

*17 top left
After 1633, the year
of Charles I's visit,
no member of the
reigning family
ever returned to
Linlithgow Palace
with the exception of
Bonnie Prince Charlie
who spent a single
night here in 1745.*

*The following year,
during the march
northwards to subdue
definitively the
residual forces of the
Jacobite rebellion,
the troops of the Duke
of Cumberland set
fire to the castle,
reducing it to its
present state.*

*17 top right Detail of
the entrance to the
palace decorated with
four colored coats of
arms, 19th-century
copies of the originals
that represented the
four knightly orders,
from right to left, The
Garter, The Thistle,
The Golden Fleece
and St. Michael.*

*16 top A portrait of
Mary Stuart, Queen of
Scotland and pretender
to the throne of Elizabeth
I. The sword, the scepter
and the jewels worn by
the Queen are today
conserved in Edinburgh
Castle.*

*16 bottom Mary Stuart
became Queen just after
her birth, because of the
death of her father,
James V. Before Mary
was three years old, the
English king Henry VIII
sent an army to demand
the fulfilment of the
marriage proposal
between his son Edward
and Mary. The episode
is known in history as
the "rough wooing."*

*16-17 Linlithgow
Palace dominates the
town and the small lake.
Although it is now
roofless, this impressive
building is still in a fair
state of preservation.
Of great beauty, its
central courtyard is
a concentration of
centuries of Scottish
history with the
extensions and additions
built at the behest of
diverse monarchs of the
Stuart dynasty. The
Stuarts were accustomed
to spending long periods
in this palace.*

M ary Queen of Scots, the heir to the powerful Stuart dynasty that had long fought against England and had brought sophisticated architecture and tastes to the Scottish court, came to the throne during the tragic years of the religious struggles between Catholics and Protestants. The daughter of James V and the French Princess, Mary of Guise, Mary Stuart had a turbulent life of love and betrayal, intrigue and assassinations that have made her a legendary figure. She was born on the 8th of December, 1542, at Linlithgow Palace, one of the Stuarts' favorite residences on the shores of the Firth of Forth, mid-way between Edinburgh and Stirling. With its powerful red towers reflecting in the water, the castle was built in 1425 by James I on his return to Scotland after eighteen years of imprisonment in England. His successors introduced modifications and refurbishments that transformed the castle into a palace rivalling those of France, as was confirmed by Queen Mary of Guise. The diverse styles of the facades facing the interior courtyard recount the history of the palace: to the east is the Great Hall and the original entrance of James I, to the north the new wing built by James IV, to the west the state apartments added by James III and to the south the English-style facade built by the sovereign and the queen Margaret Tudor.

Mary's father, James V, died of a heart attack just six days after her birth.

*18 center left and
right* At the center
of the struggle for
independence, Stirling
Castle was retaken by
the Scots in 1297
thanks to William
Wallace (photo on the
right) following the
Battle of Stirling
Bridge, then a wooden
structure linking the
north and south of
Scotland. The castle
thus became the last
Scottish fortress to
oppose Edward I.
Having been regained
by the English and
retained for ten years,
in 1324 it was again
conquered by Robert
the Bruce at the Battle
of Bannockburn
which marked a
decisive moment
for Scottish
independence.

18 bottom left
Stirling Castle was
built in its present
form between the end
of the 14th and the
16th centuries. James
IV ordered the
building of the
Great Hall and the
gatehouse. James V
on the other hand was
responsible for the
spectacular palace,
built with the help of
French masons. James
VI, at whose behest
the Royal Chapel was
built, was the last
Scottish sovereign to
reside in the castle.

18 top left and 19
Following the moat
and the first gateway
to Stirling Castle, the
road climbs to the
internal gateway.
A ramp on the left
leads to the Queen
Anne Gardens while a
third entrance opens
onto Lower Square
overlooked by the royal
palace with its
decorated facade, a
masterpiece in the
Renaissance style.
Together with the
palaces of Falkland
and Linlithgow, this is
one of the few
examples of how the
ideas of the European
Renaissance found
expression in Scotland.

The coronation of the infant Mary took place in the austere castle at Stirling where she lived until she departed for France as the fiancée of the Dauphin at just five years of age.

Set in a strategic position on the principal road linking the north and south of Scotland, Stirling was already fortified in prehistoric times. Through here passed all the Scottish kings, including Alexander I and William the Lion who also died here. Significant battles in Scottish history were fought around the castle, including that of Stirling Bridge in 1297 when the Scots, led by William Wallace, defeated the English army. Attacked on a number of occasions by the English during the wars of independence, Stirling was the last Scottish fortress to surrender in 1304. With the Stuart dynasty the castle became a royal palace, as can still be seen today. James II reinforced the defences, lending the castle its severe, invincible air, but he also constructed the Great Hall to house the Scottish Parliament and State ceremonies. James IV began work on the Renaissance-style royal palace eventually completed by his son James V who was crowned in the chapel of Stirling Castle, as was later the case with his daughter Mary and his grandson James VI in 1566.

Mary spent her childhood and youth in France in order to escape the wars with England. Educated in the luxury of the French court, in 1558 she married the Dauphin who the following year was crowned as King Francis II of France. At sixteen years of age Mary Stuart was the Queen of France and Scotland, as well as the heir to the throne of Anglican England given that her cousin Elizabeth was childless. However, a widow at eighteen, she left her mother-in-law Catherine De Medici in order to return to her homeland, a Catholic Queen in a now Protestant country.

With the exception of the inhabitants of the Highlands, the doctrines of the Protestant preacher John Knox had opened a breach in the spirit of the Scots. Charismatic and sophisticated, the young sovereign found herself at the center of political intrigues and religious power struggles. The Puritans never forgave her joie de vivre, the luxury with which she surrounded herself and her many love affairs.

20 top A view from
above of Holyrood
Palace and the ruins
of the abbey that,
legend has it, was
founded in 1128 by
David I, the son of
Malcom III and
Margaret. One day,
while out hunting,
the king was
dismounted and
wounded by a stag
but was saved by his
crucifix. He gave
thanks by
constructing the
abbey. The name
Holyrood derives
from the words Holy
and Rood, a synonym
of cross.

20-21 Holyrood Palace was built as a lodge for the abbey's guests and from the 16th century was developed into a royal residence. The lodge was made more comfortable by James IV. In 1529 the northwest tower was built to house the royal

family. This is now the oldest surviving part of the palace and was the scene of many tumultuous scenes in the life of Mary Stuart: Mary married Lord Darnley in the abbey and Bothwell in what is today the Picture Gallery.

21 top left The oldest part of the castle, the Historical Apartments, are closely tied to the history of Scotland and Mary Queen of Scots. On the first floor of the tower are the two rooms in which the queen lived and which were the scene of the brutal assassination of Davide Rizzio. The embroidery work completed by Mary during her long imprisonment in England is exhibited in a display case.

21 bottom left At the center of the large square that extends in front of the entrance to the palace stands a fountain, a 19th-century copy of the one built at Linlithgow on the occasion of the marriage of James V and Mary of Guise, the parents of Mary Queen of Scots. On the occasion of the wedding wine rather than water flowed from the spouts.

21 right The statue of the unicorn stands out on the pilasters of the gateway to Holyrood House.

Mary established her court at Holyrood Palace in Edinburgh. Built in the twelfth century as an abbey, it was transformed into a royal residence by James IV, determined to make Edinburgh the center of his kingdom. The royal apartments, decorated in the Renaissance style and richly furnished, are still today the residence of Queen Elizabeth II and Prince Philip during their visits to the city. Thanks to a pa-

pal disposition Mary Stuart married her cousin Henry Darnley in 1565. The ceremony was followed by three days of dancing and banqueting. The royal couple's chambers can still be seen in the palace, including the room in which the queen met her enemy John Knox and the one in which she spent the afternoons playing the harp, writing poetry or listening to her secretary, and perhaps her lover, Davide Rizzio from Turin. The liaison between Mary and the Italian came to a tragic end. One evening, when the Queen was in the sixth month of her pregnancy, a group of armed men sent by Darnley attacked Rizzio, who vainly tried to defend himself by clinging to the Queen. He was finished off with stab wounds, but not before having crossed the royal bedchamber dripping blood.

Holyrood Palace is also the starting point of the Royal Mile, the road that, lined by towering grey facades, climbs the hill to Edinburgh Castle. Mary took this road in the tumultuous days following the assassination of Rizzio in order to seek refuge behind the powerful walls of the castle. The symbol of Scotland is stern and apparently invincible, even though it was actually conquered on a number of occasions by the English. The oldest part of the complex is St. Margaret's Chapel, a stone building probably constructed at the behest of King David I in memory of his mother around 1130. Little remains of the ancient fortifications as they were incorporated into the extensions of the sixteenth and eighteenth centuries. The Royal Palace, the old Parliament Hall and the National War Memorial to those who fell during the Great War all overlook the interior courtyard, Crown Square. From the 16th century onwards the royal family preferred to live in more comfortable accommodation such as the palaces of Holyrood, Linlithgow and Falkland. The castle thus became the seat of government and a general military headquarter. Mary gave birth to the heir to the throne, the future James VI of Scotland, who became also James I of England after the death of Elizabeth I, in a small room on the 19th of June, 1566. She lowered the baby in a basket from a window so as to remove him from the danger of possible plots, the situation had precipitated. A plot in which Mary herself may have been involved, resulted in her second husband, Lord Darnley, being strangled. His remains were found in a building destroyed by an explosion. Three months later, to widespread disapproval, the Queen married the principal suspect of her husband's murder, James Hepburn, the Earl of Bothwell, who in the meantime had been cleared by the judges.

23 top left Built by James IV for banqueting and ceremonies, the Great Hall stands on the South side of Crown Square. Up until 1639 it was the home of the Scottish parliament, but was then transformed into barracks and subsequently a hospital. During that period the ceiling with its exposed beams was covered over, but at the end of the last century it was restored in accordance with the Romantic notions of the time.

23 top right Begun in the Renaissance style in 1430 by James IV, the royal palace was rebuilt during the time of Mary Queen of Scots to house the queen and her husband Lord Darnley, whose intertwined initials can be seen above the entrance. Mary gave birth to James VI here in a small wood-paneled room. The whole palace was rebuilt once again in 1617 when James VI, now also James I of England, made a triumphant return to Scotland. He was to be the last king to be housed in the castle.

24 top left
The massive ruins of Hermitage Castle rise isolated by a torrent on the remote moors of Liddesdale, to the north of Newcastleton. Founded in the 13th century, the castle was rebuilt 200 years later in an austere and

turreted style. Its fame is linked with the story of the Earl of Bothwell and Mary Stuart who, in order to visit her beloved wounded in a skirmish on the nearby border, did not hesitate to ride 80 miles on horseback.

The marriage, celebrated in 1567 according to the Protestant rite, was the last straw for the Scottish noblemen, who attacked the couple. The queen managed to gather troops loyal to the crown and faced the rebels at Carberry Hill near Edinburgh. After a day of heated exchanges, Mary surrendered. Isolated and rejected as a sovereign, she was imprisoned in the fourteenth-century castle of Loch Leven, today in ruins, which was built on an island in the middle of the loch. The young queen remained a prisoner for almost a year, during which time she lost the twins she was carrying, but succeeded in escaping by boat, dressed as a peasant woman after having seduced Willie Douglas, the son of the Lord of the castle. An army of six thousand men loyal to the Queen engaged in battle with the anti-Catholic faction that supported the year-old King James VI at Langside near Glasgow. They were defeated and Mary Stuart fled southwards. She spent her last night in Scotland at Dundrennan Abbey before crossing the Solway Firth and seeking the help of her cousin Elizabeth I of England. Rather than receiving support, she was imprisoned for nearly twenty years in the Tower of London before being executed in 1587.

During the seven years of her reign, Mary Stuart visited most of Scotland, staying in castles that are still associated with her name. One of the most celebrated is Hermitage Castle, a massive stone building standing isolated on the moors bordering England, where Earl Bothwell, not yet her third husband, was wounded in a skirmish. From Jedburgh, to where she had gone to superintend the hearings of the Court of Justice, the sovereign rode to her lover's aid. During the return journey she fell from her horse and lay in a coma for some days in a tower house at Jedburgh. Craigmillar Castle, one of the Queen's favorite residences, stands not far from Edinburgh. The assassination of her second husband was apparently ordered in the massive sixteenth-century central tower surrounded by two curtain walls.

24 bottom left Just a few miles separate Edinburgh and Craigmillar Castles, the latter being a brick tower with an impressive curtain wall raised in the 15th century, with additions being made over the following centuries. This castle was one of Mary Stuart's favorites and the area around it is still known as Little France after the French servants of Mary's court. It would appear that it was within these walls that the plot against Lord Darnley, Mary's second husband, was hatched.

24 top right Borthwick Castle, near Edinburgh, was built in 1430 by the 1st Lord Borthwick and is one of the most powerful fortified structures in Scotland. Mary Stuart visited the castle in 1567, shortly after her marriage to Bothwell.

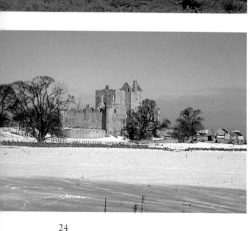

24-25 Castle Campbell stands on a rocky crag in the heart of the wooded Ochil Hills. Dating from the 15th century, this tower house was the property of Colin Campbell, the 1st Earl of Argyll and chancellor of Scotland during the early years of the reign of James IV.

In 1566 the castle was visited by the reformist preacher John Knox, Mary Stuart's great adversary. The Queen herself visited the castle in 1563. In 1645 it was conquered and burned by the Marquis of Montrose. A building in the French Renaissance style is linked to the castle.

25 top Loch Leven Castle stands on an island in a small lake at the southernmost tip of Perthshire. With its massive tower and curtain wall, it was used as an escape-proof prison from the 16th century. Mary Queen of Scots was imprisoned here for almost a year in 1567.

26 top and 26-27 Falkland Palace rises at the foot of the gentle Lomond Hills in the heart of the rich Fife Peninsula. Between 1453 and 1463 James II and Mary of Guiderdal transformed the ancient fortress into a royal palace. The current appearance of the palace dates from the 16th century and was the work of the French and Scottish master masons working for James IV and James V, respectively the grandfather and father of Mary Queen of Scots. The palace is closely associated with the life of the tragic queen. In 1542, in fact, when Mary was just a few days old, her father James V died of a heart attack.

No trace remains, however, of Dunbar Castle to where the queen fled with Lord Darnley following the assassination of Rizzio and to where she returned a few months later on her honeymoon with Bothwell. Razed to the ground by her enemies following the Battle of Carberry Hill, it was definitively destroyed by Cromwell.

Mary spent what were perhaps the happiest days of her tormented life far from the intrigues of Edinburgh in Falkland Palace, the Stuart's favorite house. Originally built as a hunting lodge, the palace was enlarged by James IV who established an elegant court there. In preparation for his marriage to the daughter of the King of France, James V transformed Falkland into a Renaissance palace with the help of master craftsmen summoned from France. The palace is set in extensive grounds that also contain the world's first tennis court.

27 left and top right
The coat of arms of the Stuarts of Bute decorates the facade of the guardhouse that defended the entrance to Falkland Palace. Completed in 1542, it housed the private apartments of Keeper, the constable and guardian of the royal palace. The 3rd Earl of Bute acquired the palace and the title of Keeper in 1887. Lord Bute undertook a restoration project that was completed in 1900.

27 bottom right
The royal borough of Falkland around the royal castle is composed of a few simple, single story stone houses. The Bruce Fountain in stone with four bright red lions stands in the square at the end of Main Street, in front of the church and the two halls designed by Thomas Barclay and built between 1800 and 1801.

27

28 top The Keeper's Bedroom on the second floor of the palace, was used by Michael Crichton Stuart and his wife Barbara when, at the end of the 2nd World War, they transformed Falkland Palace into their home. The bedroom is dominated by a four-poster bed that is said to have belonged to James VI. Superbly figured, it dates from the 17th century.

28 bottom Completely rebuilt by Lord Bute, the Drawing Room is welcoming but simple, in line with the austerity of the post-war period when it was used by Michael Crichton Stuart and his wife Barbara who was responsible for the draperies. There are portraits of James V and his second wife Mary of Lorraine, James VI, Mary Queen of Scots, Anne of Denmark, Charles II and Catherine of Braganza.

28-29 The Old Library at Falkland Palace has an elaborate ceiling with trompe l'oeil decoration dating from 1895. The room was used as a study by Michael Crichton Stuart. On the walls are a royal hunting trophy and portraits of the family, including engravings of the 3rd Earl of Bute, Prime Minister George III and the great-grandfather of the 3rd Marquis.

29 top left During the brief years of her reign, Mary Stuart initiated work on the palace and its furnishings. Like her father and her grandfather, the queen loved to escape from the oppressive atmosphere of Edinburgh, made all the more intolerable by the austerity of the Reformation, to the tranquility of Falkland. In 1562, shortly after her return from France, the queen washed the feet of 19 virgins in Falkland Chapel, a number corresponding to the years of her reign.

29 top right The Tapestry Gallery linked the royal apartments with the Chapel and the keeper's apartments. Lord Bute restored the corridor and added the oak ceiling. The gallery is covered with 17th-century Flemish tapestries acquired in Holland, that were exposed when the royal family was living in the palace.

30 top The residence of the Roxburghe family, Floors Castle is surrounded by an agricultural estate extending over 56,000 acres along the banks of the River Tweed. The estate is composed of 50 tenanted farms, two grouse moors, 3,900 acres of woodland, a golf course, a thoroughbred stud farm and salmon fishing reserves.

30-31 Built on a cliff dropping sheer to the sea, Tantallon Castle was considered to be impregnable as it was protected from attack by land by a double moat. Direct attacks and even incendiary arrows in fact failed to conquer the castle and it surrendered only in 1661 after 12 days of bombardment by Cromwell's troops under the leadership of General Monk.

Southern Scotland is a region of golden hills, fields bordered by high hedges, stately homes and ruined abbeys, but also of forests and bleak heather-covered hills recalling those of the Highlands. The areas bordering England, to the south of the Scottish capital of Edinburgh, rarely enjoyed long periods of tranquility. From the incursions of the Roman legions until the Act of Union, the valley of the River Tweed and the Pentland and Moorfoot Hills were the theaters of savage and bloody battles. One of the most disastrous was the Battle of Flodden Field of 1513 in which the Scots were routed by the English army and James IV was killed. The Scottish king's year-old son succeeded him as James V, the future father of Mary Queen of Scots. In these turbulent lands, the castles represented the Scots' defensive kingpins. In the city of Harwick, close to the border, are the remains of one of the country's oldest defensive structures: an artificially raised earth mound that was once protected by palisades and on which stood a wooden lookout and defensive tower. At the foot of the tower a palisade protected houses and their inhabitants. No trace of the tower remains, but the Motte, the artificial mound, is still today the focal point of the Common Ridings, the costumed reconstructions that commemorate the site's tumultuous history. The ruins of Tantallon Castle standing above a rocky cliff at the mouth of the Firth of Forth are some of the most evocative in

31 top The present-day appearance of Abbotsford, the home of Sir Walter Scott, dates from 1853 when the West Wing with the chapel, the kitchen and the servants' quarters was added. When Scott was alive he received in this house Maria Edgeworth, Wordsworth, Thomas Moore and Washington Irving. After the writer's death Queen Victoria visited Abbotsford and took tea with the family.

31 bottom The west facade of Hopetoun House overlooks the great park on the shores of the Firth of Forth, criss-crossed by nature trails open to the public. The hand of the architect William Bruce can be seen in the linearity of the facade.

32 top and 32-33 Set close to Edinburgh, Dalmeny House is the Gothic Revival home of the Earls of Rosebery and is filled with French furniture and paintings by Gainsborough, Reynolds and Lawrence. The house stands in extensive grounds that reach the seashore and within which pheasants with beautiful colored plumage wander undisturbed and sheep graze on the roadsides.

33 The home of the Hay family since 1696, Duns Castle stands in the southern part of the Borders region. The current owner has restored the castle to make it more comfortable without altering the characteristics of its rich past. The lake and grounds are particularly fine. The photos show the dining room and a detail of the exterior.

the whole of Scotland. Built in the fourteenth century by the Douglas family in red sandstone, Tantallon was the last Medieval castle with curtain walls and an entrance tower to be constructed in Scotland. The austere and isolated Traquair House standing in the Tweed Valley is even older and its history is linked with that of Mary Queen of Scots and Bonnie Prince Charlie. In spite of its position close to the border and the unwavering devotion of its owners to the Stuarts, the castle has survived to the threshold of the new millennium virtually intact. The estate is still inhabited by the original owners who belong to a branch of the Stuart family. Thirlestane is another castle still inhabited by its owners, although its Medieval core has been extended and rebuilt over the centuries. At the end of the eighteenth century, following the Union with England, the region settled into a period of prosperity. The economic well-being resulting from the nascent industries led to a flourishing of the arts, architecture and literature. The area's most famous figures were no longer the representatives of the old aristocracy, but rather architects such as William and Robert Adam and poets and writers such as Robert Burns and Walter Scott. Edinburgh became a center of the arts and expanded with fine new quarters constructed in the Georgian style. The great Borders and Lothian estates also saw the construction of numerous mansions surrounded by parks and gardens. Among the most important were Hopetoun

House on the western edge of Edinburgh and Mellerstain House, set between the River Tweed and the Cheviot Hills. Both were fruit of the Adam family genius. The initial designs by William Adam were subsequently developed by his sons, in particular Robert. William Adam was also responsible for the original design of Floors Castle, located close to the town of Kelso, amplified a century later by the architect Playfair. Floors Castle is today the largest inhabited castle in Scotland and was chosen as a location for the film *Greystoke*, in which it was the home of Tarzan. The revival of the legends of the Highlands influenced the country houses constructed by the great landowners of the Lowlands during the last century such as Dalmeny House, overlooking the Firth of Forth, or Abbotsford House, the beloved home of Sir Walter Scott, the writer and creator of the myth of romantic Scotland.

Surrounded by a large park on the South bank of the Firth of Forth, just a few miles out of Edinburgh, Hopetoun House was originally built by Sir William Bruce, the architect of Holyrood Palace, for the 1st Earl of Hopetoun, Charles Hope. The estate had been acquired in 1678 by his father John Hope, a descendant of a family of traders and judges. Unfortunately, John was never

able to live on the new property as he died in a shipwreck while accompanying the Duke of York, the future James VII of Scotland (James II of England). Work on the house began in 1699 with the construction of a central body that was extended in 1712 by William Adam and, following his death in 1748, by his three sons, John, Robert and James who were responsible for the decoration of the interiors between 1752 and 1767. The result is highly effective even though the hands of the different architects can be detected. The western facade with the classical central body is the work of Bruce. In contrast, the eastern facade, with the curving colonnades linking the wings to the central body is a theatrical stroke of genius by William Adam, undoubtedly one of his masterpieces. Inside the house, the staircases and the wooden paneling with inlaid flowers and fruits are by Bruce, while the salons with their stuccoed and gilded ceilings display the neo-classical touch of the Adams. Paintings by artists of the caliber of Rubens, Titian and Canaletto can be seen throughout the house, acquired by members of the family during the frequent foreign trips customarily taken in the last centuries by young members of the noble families. The opulent house was not inhabited throughout the year, however. The members of the family would spend weeks at the spa in Bath or would stay London while they enjoyed court life when they were not traveling in the direction of Paris or Rome. John MacKay,

34 top The Red Drawing Room is the only room in the house to retain its original function. The gilded stucco work of the ceiling is one of the most magnificent examples of Rococo decoration in Scotland and was the work of John Dawson. The red damask wallpaper dates from 1766. The furniture was made to measure to be set against the walls. In the 18th century, in fact, the room was used for entertaining. Only occasionally were small tables placed in the room. The white marble Italian fireplace features neo-classical decoration. The sofas and armchairs are upholstered in red damask.

34 bottom The staircase is undoubtedly the principal feature of the house designed by Bruce. The pine panels are carved with floral and fruit motifs, the work of Alexander Eizat who had already worked with Bruce at Holyrood Palace. The banister rail is carved from oak. On the walls hang the paintings commissioned to William McLaren in 1967 by the 3rd Marquis of Linlithgow in memory of his wife.

34-35 and 35 top
The western facade of
the Georgian house is
reflected in the waters
of the lake. The
grounds offer broad
views of the shore of
the Firth
of Forth and the hills
of the Fife peninsula.
In early spring the

grounds are ablaze
with thousands of
daffodils followed by
primroses, bluebells
and, in early
summer by
rhododendrons and
azaleas. The extent of
the park can be
appreciated in the
aerial view (top).

36 top left
Sir William Bruce designed this bedroom for the young 1st Duke. It is composed of a series of three chambers including a dressing room and wardrobe. The wall covering with gilded decorations is the work of James Norrie of Edinburgh.

36 bottom left
The oak panels of this bedroom have led to it becoming known as the Wainscot Bed Chamber. The decoration dates from the early 17th century, with a series of wallpapers from Antwerp datable to the same period.

36 center right The current Great Library is composed of numerous small, inter-connecting rooms that were originally used as bedrooms or writing rooms. The rebuilding and redesignation of the rooms was the work of Adam in 1720. The library features books collected by the

family with works on archaeology, law, philosophy, religion and European history. The environment is austere but very welcoming with the walls fully lined with wood and perfectly preserved books. In the middle of the room stands a billiards table.

36 top right
The Yellow Drawing Room occupies the original dining room. The stucco-work on the ceiling is by John Dawson and the door and window frames

are by John Paterson, while the furniture in the Rococo style is by James Cullen. The yellow damask silk covering the walls is the original 1850 covering.

in his *Journey Through Scotland* published in 1728, writes, "The attractive palace and gardens are set in a great park, full of deer and surrounded by a stone walls. To the south of the main road there is the vegetable garden and close by the lodge for pheasants. Below the Earl's great terrace there is an oyster farm so that the kitchen can be supplied in great quantities throughout the year." On the 29th of August, 1822, Sir John Hope, the 4th Earl of Hopetoun, welcomed George IV to his home during his visit to Scotland, the first sovereign to set foot in the country after Charles II. The road from South Queensferry was completely repaved for the occasion and the gates of Hopetoun were opened to allow the people to see the king.

The Hope family created a charitable trust in 1974 to ensure the preservation of Hopetoun House, opening the main rooms to the public and reserving a wing of the house for themselves. During the summer months the house provides a magnificent setting for recitals of classical music.

36 bottom right The service room was created at the same time as the State Dining Room while a large kitchen was fitted out on the floor below. This photo shows

the system of bells used to call servants from the various rooms. Hot dishes were carried from the kitchen to the dining room in a steam-heated container.

37 The State Dining Room was designed in the 19th century by the architect James Gillespie Graham. It is a sophisticated and thorough example of the late period Regency style with original decor and furnishings such as the gilded stucco work of the frieze, the large

rayed medallion of the chandelier, the fireplace, the gold wall coverings and the elaborate drapes. The great mahogany table dates from 1820. There are numerous paintings on the wall including a portrait of the Countess of Hopetoun by Gainsborough.

THIRLESTANE CASTLE

38 top left In 1840 this large drawing room was extended by incorporating the music room that opened off the original drawing room. The room presents a magnificent stuccoed ceiling with laurel wreaths and garlands of flowers and fruit. The tall mirrors in gilded frames reflect the decoration of the ceiling and make the room very luminous.

38 bottom left The dining room is situated in the South Wing, added to the original central buiding. The stuccoed ceiling is by James Annan and the red walls are literally covered with portraits of the family, one of the richest picture galleries of any Scottish castle.

The ancient royal village of Lauder, to the South of Edinburgh, is famous for hosting one of the oldest Common Ridings, the historical reconstructions of the cavalry skirmishes that took place throughout the Borders region. Thirlestane Castle stands on the bank of the River Leader and has been the home of the Maitland family from the sixteenth century to

the present day. The castle boasts the most imposing and diversified facade of any in Scotland, with a host of symmetrical round or square towers and turrets, topped by parapets or pinnacles. The original tower, incorporated into the present building in pinkish stone with grey slate roofs, dates back to 1225. It was transformed into a residence by William, the secretary of Mary Queen of Scots. His brother John, the 1st Duke of Maitland, secretary and Chancellor to James VI, transformed it into a luxurious home with an oblong structure in red stone and a circular tower at each corner. A century later his grandson, the Duke of Lauderdale whose ghost is said to still haunt the castle, worked on the extension of Thirlestane with the royal architect Sir William Bruce, responsible for the rebuilding of Holyrood Palace in Edinburgh. Bruce added two massive square towers to which David Bryce in turn added two wings in dark stone during the last century. The interiors were renewed during the Victorian period, preserving the ceilings decorated with stucco-work from the sixteenth century. The castle also features the attractive old kitchens, and a nursery with a collection of antique toys including model soldiers, puppets, dolls, rocking horses and dolls' houses. The Borders Country Life Museum deals with the domestic life, agriculture and sport of the past centuries.

38 top right In 1840 the castle's kitchen was incorporated into the new South Wing where it continued to operate as we see it today until the end of the Second World War. The center of the room is dominated by the great work table. A laundry was created in the adjacent rooms.

38-39 The complex facade of Thirlestane Castle, the result of successive extensions, appears in all its beauty in the light of the sun that emphasizes the different color of the stone and accentuates the movement of the structure dominated by the tall central tower.

40 top left The magnificent portrait of Lady Grisell Hume, the wife of George Baillie, by Maria Varelst. Lady Grisell is the most important figure in the history of Mellerstain. When she was a girl of just twelve years of age she carried secret messages written by her father Sir Patrick Hume to his friend Baillie who was imprisoned in the Tolbooth in Edinburgh.

MELLERSTAIN HOUSE

This large Georgian house is another of the Scottish masterpieces by the Adam architects, and it can be considered as a symbol of the architectural canons of the era: first and foremost the integration of architecture and natural beauty. The austere lines of the facade thus echo those of the Italianate garden with its terraces that descend towards the lake and the slopes of the Cheviot Hills in the background. The principal entrance overlooks green lawns, shrubs and low trees that grow denser as they approach the edge of the woods. Mellerstain House was constructed in two phases. The first two low wings with the tranquil charm of country cottages were designed by William Adam in 1725. The broad central block was completed forty-five years later, between 1770 and 1778, by his son, the famous architect Robert Adam: austere Gothic lines, yellow stone and battlements as the only concession to decoration. The house was built for the Baillies of Jerviswood, descendants of the rich Edinburgh merchant George Baillie who had bought the estate in 1742 and who had lived until his death in a large old house called Whiteside that stood not far from the present Mellerstain House. Many years were to pass before his grandson, who was also called George, after years of exile in Holland and economic privations, managed to return to his homeland in the retinue of the Prince of Orange, King William III.

42 top Luminous and welcoming, the small library occupies chambers that were originally designed as dressing rooms. The decor is the work of Robert Adam and dates from 1778. Among the pictures hanging on the walls is a portrait of Thomas, 6th Duke of Haddington by Sir Godfrey Kneller.

42-43 A masterpiece of Palladian architecture, the library is full of classical references, beginning with the four long panels placed above the bookshelves with figures in white stucco against a dark green background. The scenes depict classical motifs such as the Nine Muses, the Sacrifice of Iphigenia, the Labors of Hercules and the Pleading of Priam for the Body of Hector.

43 top The Great Gallery is a long room that houses a small museum with objects collected by the family over the last two centuries. The ceiling was designed by Robert Adam, but never completed. Among the paintings on the wall is The Burgomaster Le Blom of Antwerp attributed to Van Dyck.

43 bottom The Stone Hall features a William Adam fireplace with precious Delft ceramic tiles. The landscape above the fireplace depicts the River Tweed at Kelso and was painted by R. Norrie in 1725. The round table dates from the Victorian period. Helmets and halberds complete the furnishings.

The Mellerstain estate was restored to its rightful owner and work began on the construction of a new house built to the designs of William Adam. George Baillie's wife, Lady Grisell Hume, became a legendary figure and her *Household Book* is considered a classic text providing insights into the social life of the era. On her death it was another grandson, George Haddington Baillie, who was responsible for completing the construction as we see it today.

Inspired by the classical architecture he had seen while on the Grand Tour through Greece and Italy he chose Robert Adam as his architect. The hand of the maestro is evident in the decoration of the elegant interiors which still today retain their original pastel colors and the ceilings decorated with stuccowork and medallions. The high point is the library with a play of pastel colors (pale green, pink, a bluish grey and ivory) in which the stucco decorations, the medallions, the bookshelves and the panels with classical figures are inserted. On the second floor is another of Adam's masterpieces, the Great Gallery with its Ionic columns. In this case, however, the ceiling was never finished. It remains a mystery as to what such a vast and sumptuous room in such an isolated part of the house was intended to be used as. It can only be reached via a secondary staircase and through a salon in the Oriental style. Mellerstain House also boasts a fine collection of antique furniture and paintings, among which is a Van Dyck.

FLOORS CASTLE

44 top *Floors Castle is surrounded by gardens and a park designed by William Adam. However, prior to the transformation of the house, the formal gardens were also extended, being transformed into an open park reaching the bank of the River Tweed.*

44-45 *On the north side can still be seen the original central body designed by William Adam, to which were added the lateral towers and the two wings which repeat to a smaller scale the symmetrical design of the central element.*

*F*loors Castle, set on a natural terrace at the foot of the Cheviot Hills, stands at the center of an estate in the Tweed valley, a few miles from the town of Kelso. Work on its construction began in 1721 at the behest of John, the 1st Duke of Roxburghe, an active promoter of the Act of Union, who commissioned William Adam to enlarge the earlier fortified castle and to create a residence in the Georgian style. All that remains of the great architect's design is a painting by William Wilson hanging in the sitting room.

James, the 6th Duke, had Adam's building "embellished" and in 1849 the architect William Playfair gave free reign to his imagination and talent, adding such a quantity of turrets, spires and cupolas as to make the castle resemble, according to a comment by Sir Walter Scott, that of Oberon and Titiana, the king and queen in Shakespeare's *Midsummer Night's Dream*. Early this century, thanks to the marriage of the 8th Duke to a rich American heiress, May Goelets, Floors Castle was endowed with an important art collection.

In the 1930s diverse modifications were made to the interior, in particular to the sitting room and the ballroom which were completely refurbished in order to exhibit the Brussels and Gobelins tapestries.

45 top *The entrance hall is dominated by the portrait of the 3rd Duke painted in Rome by Pompeo Batoni in 1761-1762. Above the fireplace there is a large painting by Hendrick Danckerts that shows Charles II strolling with his court in Horse Guards Parade. In the background can be seen Whitehall. At the center of the room stands an oak table with lion's paw feet.*

45 bottom *This attractive room was refurnished by Duchess May in 1930 to make it less formal. On the walls can be seen a recent portrait of the present Duke by Howard Morgan, and a painting of Floors Castle in the design by William Adam. There is a small water-color of Kelso signed by Turner on the small table alongside the fireplace.*

46 The great
ballroom was
designed by Playfair
in 1842 and enjoys a
broad view over the
river. In the 1930s
Duchess May covered

the 19th-century
decorations with oak
panels on which hang
18th-century Gobelins
tapestries depicting
Neptune, Ceres, Venus,
Cupid and Juno.

47 Designed as a
billiards room by the
architect Playfair, this
room was subsequently
converted into a
dining room. It today
houses a rich
collection of
silverware, including
the cutlery created by

Paul Stort in 1819
and the cups with
gilded silver handles
made by Paul de
Lamerie in 1726.
Among the portraits
hanging on the walls
is one of the actress
Peg Woffington by
Hogarth.

48 top In 1831, at
sixty years of age, Sir
Walter Scott
undertook a journey
to the Mediterranean,
visiting Malta,
Naples and Rome in
the hope of regaining
his health. He

returned to
Abbotsford House the
following June but
was very ill. He had
his bed carried into
the dining room
where he died gazing
out at his beloved
river.

ABBOTSFORD HOUSE

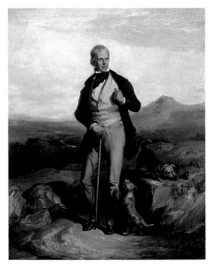

The valley of the River Tweed was the area of Scotland beloved of Sir Walter Scott, the writer whose novels contributed to the nineteenth-century fashion for romantic Scotland and to the revival of bagpipes and kilts that had been virtually abandoned following the defeat at Culloden. He had been aware of the beauty of the region ever since his childhood spent on his grandfather's farm at Sandyknowe close to Mellerstain House. When, in 1799, he was appointed Sheriff of Selkirk he was able to settle definitively in the Borders. In 1812 he acquired Cartleyhole Farm where he began work on a series of new novels including *Waverley* and *Rob Roy*. Ten years later he demolished the old farmhouse and began work on Abbotsford House, so named in commemoration of the fact that the land had once belonged to the wealthy Melrose Abbey. The new building with its turrets and battlements was designed by William Atkinson in imitation of a Scottish baronial castle of the previous centuries. Typically, Scott turned the house into a concentration of elements symbolizing Scottish Romanticism, from the sword said to have belonged to the outlaw hero Rob Roy MacGregor to a reproduction of the portal of the nearby abbey. In the library, a large room overlooking the river, the walls are lined with the 9,000 volumes collected by the writer, while the ceiling is an exact replica of the one in the chapel at Rosslyn.

48 center and bottom Abbotsford House is a distillation of 19th-century Scottish Romanticism. A lover of the legendary past of Scotland, the writer was in fact proud of his homeland and an enthusiastic expert on the heroes of the Highlands such as Rob Roy or the glorious William Wallace, of whom he collected relics and mementoes.

48-49 Surrounded by greenery, Abbotsford House, seen in this aerial photo, is a triumph of Gothic Revival decoration. It houses the Scott Museum which recounts the life of the novelist and exhibits many of the objects he collected during his lifetime or received as gifts.

49 top In 1812 Sir Walter Scott moved with his family to Cartleyhole and between 1817 and 1821 extended the small farm until it reached the size of the present-day Abbotsford House, of which the facade overlooking the river can be seen here. In 1830, when the writer was declared bankrupt, his creditors allowed him to keep the estate.

50 top The library is the most beautiful room in Abbotsford House, overlooking the River Tweed. The over nine thousand volumes are arranged around the walls. Some of them carry the legend "Clausus Tutus Ero" engraved on the spine, an anagram of Gualterus Scotus. The ceiling was deliberately copied from the one destroyed in the Abbey at Rosslyn.

50-51 The entrance hall at Abbotsford is panelled in oak. Some of the panels are finely carved and came from the Auld Kirk in Dunfermline. Others actually came from Holyrood Palace. In this room one can also admire armor, helmets and other objects collected personally by Sir Walter Scott on the battlefield at Waterloo.

51 top left Between the drawing room and the dining room lies the small armory which in Scott's day was used as a smokers' corridor and now contains a vast collection of pistols and swords, including a Highlands broad sword. Some of the objects are associated with Rob Roy, the legendary Scottish hero and protagonist in one of Scott's novels.

51 top right Sir Walter Scott died on the 21st of September, 1832, in the dining room, which is still used today for family meals. "It was such a quiet day, that the sound he loved most, the gentle murmur of the voice of the Tweed over its pebbles could clearly be heard while we were gathered around his bed," wrote his son-in-law Walter Lockhart.

51 center right Not accessible to the public, the private study is full of memories and relics of the family. The descendants of Sir Walter Scott still live in the 19th-century house although it has now been opened to the public.

51 bottom right Sir Walter Scott's writing desk was made as a copy of the one owned by his friend John Morrit using wood from a ship of the Spanish Armada. In this room the writer, who collected ancient Scottish poems and stories so as to rewrite them in the form of ballads and novels, produced some of his historical novels.

TRAQUAIR HOUSE

Massive and imposing, with small windows and two low wings, Traquair House is the oldest continuously inhabited building in the whole of Scotland. Its origins are lost in the mists of the first millennium, although it is first documented in 1107 when it was used as a lodge by Alexander I when hunting in Ettrick Forest. Alexander was the first of a long line of Scottish kings who stayed at Traquair and it remained a royal residence until the thirteenth century. During the reign of David I, the successor to Alexander, local laws were proclaimed, justice was dispensed and assemblies of the clan chieftains were held at Traquair. Many of the Traquair Charters, such as those signed by King William the Lion which granted the status of city to Glasgow, are still preserved in the castle and are exhibited to the public in rotation in the museum room and the library. On the death of Alexander III in 1286 the oldest dynasty of Scottish kings was extinguished and the period of peace in the Borders was interrupted. During the war for independence Traquair became a strategic element in the defensive system thanks to its position on the riverbank. The course of the Tweed was actually diverted in the mid-seventeenth century by the first Earl of Traquair in order to prevent damp from undermining the foundations of the castle. Occupied by the English during the reigns of Edward I and II, the castle returned to Scottish hands thanks to Robert the Bruce. Then, for 150 years the property passed from one owner to another as the political climate shifted. When James III came to the throne in 1460 he granted Traquair to his favorite Robert Lord Boyd. In 1478 the uncle of the King, the Duke of Buchan, became the owner. It was then inherited by the Duke's brother James Stuart, an ancestor of the current owners. The Stuarts of Traquair supported Mary Queen of Scots and, subsequently, the Jacobite cause. The castle thus became a haven for Catholic priests, as demonstrated by the priest's hole, accessed by

52 top and 52-53 Traquair House, the oldest inhabited house in Scotland, is surrounded by a luxuriant garden overlooking the River Tweed. During the religious wars a Catholic priest was concealed in the house in a secret room that can still be seen on the third floor, adjacent to the library where religious services were held.

52 bottom A soft rug, two sofas and an armchair in front of the fireplace lend the Lower Drawing Room a warm, welcoming atmosphere. The mirror above the fireplace and the paintings flanking it on the same wall are particularly fine.

53 top The High Drawing Room conserves a simple, tranquil appearance, with white sofas, doors and walls and a collection of portraits of women: Christian Anstruther, the wife of the 6th Earl of Traquair, Lady Isobel and Lady Jean Seton painted by Cornelius Jansen. Gilded panels and decorations are set above the doors and the fireplace. In a corner of the room is a harpsichord by Andreas Ruckers from 1651.

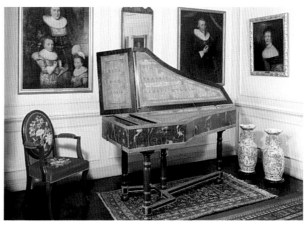

54 top left In large old houses such as Traquair, servants were often summoned by a complex system of bells connecting every room. Generally the bells were placed in a passageway between the kitchen and the pantry so that they could be heard by the entire staff.

54 top right Family portraits are hung on the walls of the sober dining room in the South Wing of the house. Set above the fireplace is a portrait of the 1st Earl of Traquair. On his left is the Jacobite 5th Earl, Charles. Among the women is the 4th Countess of Traquair, Medina who had 17 children.

54-55 Set on the third floor, the austere library dates from the middle of the 18th century. The walls are lined with antique and rare volumes still carrying their old catalogue numbers. The painted frieze framing the ceiling features busts of major figures from antiquity.

55 top The old laundry is in reality a small museum of objects from the past, from old cast-iron flat-irons to coal scuttles. The most unusual piece is an old mangle from 1840, that was once used to smooth and iron the clothes.

55 center and bottom The royal bed chamber is dominated by a sumptuous yellow four-poster bed in which it is said that Mary Stuart once slept. Legend has it that the bedspread is the work of the queen and her ladies-in-waiting, the four Maries. It is also said that the cradle was used for James VI, the future James I of England. The portrait close to the window is of Lady Ann Seton, the wife of the 2nd Earl of Traquair. The adjacent room is the dressing room with a bath and toilet necessities.

a secret flight of steps, in which it is said that a cleric was concealed for no less than sixty years.

In 1566 Mary Queen of Scots stayed at Traquair with Lord Darnley. A blanket embroidered by Mary and her ladies-in-waiting remains as evidence of her passing. The ceremonial entrance, the Bear Gate, named after the bears decorating the pilasters, has been locked since 1745 when the Earl of the day wished good luck to Bonnie Prince Charlie and swore that it would not be opened until the Stuarts had been returned to the throne.

The present appearance of Traquair House is the result of diverse transformations executed principally during the fifteenth and seventeenth centuries. The defensive tower of the ancient Scottish kings has been incorporated into the mansion house; in the mid-16th century a new wing was added with a rectangular tower protecting the West side, while another wing dates from the end of the seventeenth century.

Inside the house there are collections of ceramics and porcelain, portraits of local noblemen, the beds in which royalty slept during their stays and a beautiful library with a wealth of antique books which are not in the best of condition due to the damp. The chapel is decorated with wooden bas-reliefs from Flanders. The cellars house a collections of tools and the fascinating system of bells used to summon servants. Traquair House boasts an ancient but still active brewery in which beer is produced using traditional methods.

56 top
The general symmetry
of Drumlanrig Castle
is also seen in the
details such as the
windows, the chimneys
and the turrets.
The fascinating 17th-
century building in
pink stone is
surrounded by a large
park delimited by the
wild Dumfrieshire
Hills.

56-57 Built in 1270
and extended over
the course of the
centuries,
Caerlaverock Castle
features three corner
towers, one of which
has been completely
destroyed. The
entrance on the north
side gives an
impression of great
solidity but the castle
was nonetheless
conquered by the
English immediately
after construction
had been completed.

I rish monks brought Christianity to the land of the Picts and the Scots by way of this rugged coastline in which the border between lake and sea is uncertain. Tradition has it that they brought with them the Stone of Destiny which has ever since symbolized the power of the Crown and upon which the kings and queens of Great Britain are still crowned in Westminster Abbey. From the fifth century onwards the Celts joined forces with the local peoples to create the small kingdom of Dalriada. The royal capital was a fortress perched on the hill of Dunadd and surrounded by water and marshes. Today, on the crag that overlooks the wilderness of Crinan Moss, all that remains are ruined walls, a hollowed stone and a panel with inscriptions in *ogham*, the oldest form of Celtic writing, all symbols of the coronation ceremony. Tradition has it that in 574, St. Columba crowned King Aidan, perhaps the first Christian ceremony to be held in the British Isles. The raids of the Vikings and their settlement on the coast that so closely resembled their native fjords, slowly eroded the power of the tiny kingdom. The capital was moved to Dunstaffnage, to the North of Oban, where in 850 Kenneth MacAlpine took steps to fuse his kingdom with that of the Picts, transferring the court and the Stone of Destiny to Scone in Central Scotland. In 1060 with Malcom Canmore, the region became part of the Kingdom of Scotland albeit retaining a degree of independence thanks to the power of the local nobles. During the twelfth century a chieftain from Morven, Somerled, married the daughter of a Norwegian king thus obtaining vastly increased power and giving rise through his three descendants to the diverse branches of the MacDonald clan. Towards the end of the century the head of the Campbell clan was Cailen Mor of Loch Awe whose descendants became the dukes, earls and marquises of Argyll. The relative autonomy of the region with respects to the Crown continued until 1455 when James II took Threave Castle, the home of the Douglas clan, the Lords of Galloway. This five-story tower house was built on an island in the River Dee by the 3rd Earl of Douglas between 1369 and 1390. Dating from the late thirteenth century is Caerlaverock Castle, a fortress with an unusual triangular plan surrounded by a moat, austere on the outside but with an internal courtyard elegantly decorated with Renaissance motifs. Following the wars for independence there was a long period of internal conflict as the various clans struggled for power and land, at times supporting, at others rebelling against the Scottish Crown. The most tragically famous episode was that of the massacre of the MacDonalds by the Lords of Argyll, the Campbells. The government in England had set a date, the 31st of December, 1691, for the definitive submission of the clans to the Crown. The MacDonalds of Glen Coe reached Fort William late and were unable to find the magistrate authorized to hear their oath of allegiance. They thus journeyed to Inveraray to swear the oath. The paperwork arrived in Edinburgh just a few days late but this was sufficient to provoke extremely severe punishment: on the 13th of February 1692 at Glen Coe over 200 persons were massacred including women, old people and children. The castle of the Dukes of

Argyll, the leaders of the Campbell clan, is located at Inveraray and in its present form with turrets and false battlements dates from the eighteenth century. Culzean Castle, an elegant neo-classical mansion by Robert Adam overlooking the sea, dates from the same era and is surrounded by a large park. Another great Scottish architect, Sir William Bruce, was responsible for the design of Drumlanrig Castle, in the heart of Dumfries and Galloway, a region in the Southwest of Scotland. Brodick Castle on the island of Arran is the result of repeated and successive extensions, the last of which dates from the mid-Victorian period.

58 top Dunstaffnage Castle stands on a rocky promontory dominating Loch Etive. The current building dates from the 13th century and presents a powerful curtain wall and three defensive towers. In the mid-18th century it became the prison of Flora MacDonald, the woman from Skye who aided the escape of the unfortunate Bonnie Prince Charlie, the last of the Stuart dynasty to lay claim to the Scottish throne.

58 bottom Romantic
and imposing, in spite
of being partially
ruined, Threave
Castle is reached by
boat across the River
Dee. Following the
battle of Flodden
Field a defensive ring
with walls and towers
was added. Only the
bare walls remained
after the Covenanters'
siege of 1640.

58-59 Bothwell
Castle in Strathclyde
is the most beautiful
and largest of the
13th-century Scottish
castles. It was fought
over at length during
the wars of
independence. Part
of the original
circular tower still
exists today,
although the
majority of the castle
is the result of
additions made
during the 14th and
15th centuries.

INVERARAY CASTLE

*I*nveraray is a village built during the eighteenth century on the shores of Loch Fyne, close to the mouth of the River Aray from which it takes its name. Developed on a cross-shaped plan, the castle is a perfect example of neo-classical architecture. It was commissioned by Archibald, the 3rd Duke of Argyll, who established an ambitious plan to replace the crumbling Medieval castle built in 1457 by his ancestor Colin. In order to create the new stately home and the grounds that were to surround it, the old village was demolished and completely rebuilt a short distance away. The work was completed between 1770 and 1780 in the face of myriad difficulties given that at that

time there were no viable roads within forty miles. The new residence of the Campbells, the Dukes of Argyll, one of Scotland's most powerful families who led the Covenanters during the religious wars of the mid-seventeenth century, was designed by the architect Roger Morris of the Palladian school. The symmetrical appearance of the building was, however, modified during the last century when, following a fire, the corner towers were capped and garrets were added, topped with minuscule tympanums in an incredible medley of styles. The resulting building features turrets like those of fairy-tale castles and magnificently decorated halls. The best of these is the great dining hall with colored ornamental motifs painted in 1784 by the French painters Girard and Gruinard.

62 One of a pair of geese from the Chinese Chi'en Lung dynasty (1736-1795) exhibited in the dining room. This goose is holding a fish in its beak, while its pair has an eel. The two ceramic sculptures were used as soup tureens. Along with the miniature cannon in embossed silver and gold they are among the rarest pieces in the castle.

S et between the peninsula of Kintyre and the West Coast, the small island of Arran is dominated by the peak of Goat Fell. At its foot, overlooking Brodick Bay, stands a romantic Victorian-looking ivy-covered castle built in red stone. Surrounded by luxuriant grounds, up until 1957 the castle was the home of the Dukes of Hamilton in which they studied, gardened and received guests in a very informal atmosphere. On the death of the last owner, Duchess Mary Louise of Montrose, the castle passed to the state and thence to the National Trust for Scotland. The castle was built in the thirteenth century on the ruins of an earlier Viking fortress. However, only parts of the base of this Medieval tower, once of strategic importance in the defence of the Clyde estuary, have survived.

62-63 and 63 top In the photo appears the avenue leading to Brodick Castle, an elegant Victorian manor house with ancient Medieval origins. Around the castle extends a large formal garden with flower beds and rhododendrons planted by the last Duchess of Montrose. In 1980 the woods of Brodick Castle became the first natural park in the Scottish islands managed by the Countryside Commission for Scotland. The woods are inhabited by squirrels, peregrine falcons and even the golden eagle.

*64 bottom left
The kitchen is large
and airy, equipped
with two hearths,
three ovens and an
original spit driven
by a water wheel.
Almost the entire
battery of copper pans
is original, with just
a few pieces being
added recently. Much
of the pewter is
stamped with the
symbol of the
Hamilton family.*

*64 top right The
Drawing Room is the
largest room in the
castle and is located in
the Victorian wing
added in 1844. It
contains a number of
examples of superb
craftsmanship from
candelabras to
ceramics, as well as a
number of
magnificent paintings
including the portrait
of the Duchess of
Montrose by De Laszlo.*

On the death of William, the 2nd Duke of Hamilton, at the Battle of Worcester, Cromwell's troops occupied the castle in 1652 and a new wing was added. In spite of the successive interventions, the castle was not inhabited by the family until the end of the last century when, on the crest of the wave of interest in the Highlands and attracted by the wealth of game, the Hamiltons decided not to develop the estate which actually represented a minor part of their patrimony centering on Hamilton Palace in Lanarkshire. In 1843 Alexander, the 10th Duke, commissioned an extension to the castle on the occasion of the marriage of his son William, the future 11th Duke, and the German princess Mary of Baden, a cousin of Napoleon. The design of the new wing, to the west of the old tower, was entrusted to

James Gillespie Graham, one of the architects of Edinburgh's New Town. The result is a castle of baronial appearance in which the new elements fuse perfectly with the old and the linear design of the fenestration contrasts harmoniously with the battlements and the gargoyles of the roof. Gillespie was responsible for the entrance hall, dark and imposing, with arms and hunting trophies along with an oak fireplace inlaid with the family's coat of arms. The castle houses a rich collection of silver, porcelain and paintings, including works by Watteau and Turner, part of the remarkable collection of William Beckford, father-in-law of the 10th Duke. There is also an attractive library with equestrian prints on the walls, and a kitchen with an exceptional battery of copper pans. In the castle grounds, the walled garden dates from 1710, but the true masterpiece is the rhododendron garden established by the Countess of Montrose and considered to be one of the most beautiful anywhere in Great Britain with dozens and dozens of diverse varieties. There is also an interesting ice room that was packed with snow gathered from the mountains or imported from Canada during the winter to provide a year-round supply for the conservation of food before the introduction of refrigerators. In 1980, the woodlands on the estate were declared a Country Park with 10 miles of marked footpaths along the Hamilton and Montrose families' favorite walks.

64-65 Situated in the 16th-century wing, the dining room is a majestic and imposing space. The ceiling in white stucco dates from 1844, while the wood paneling which came from Letheringham Abbey in Suffolk was installed in 1920. Above the fireplace hangs a painting by Philip Reinagle depicting the struggle between William Warr and William Wood at Nevestock in 1788. Each year the table is laid according to a family tradition, using silverware and porcelain belonging to the Beckford and Hamilton collections.

65 top left The entrance hall was built in 1844 to the designs of the architect James Gillespie Graham. The coat of arms of the Duke of Hamilton is carved in oak above the fireplace. The furniture is mainly Victorian, although in some cases the wood used to make it came from the existing furnishings. A collection of hunting trophies is displayed in the hall and along the stairs, with 87 heads of deer hunted on the island. There is also a fine collection of sporting scenes by James Pollard.

65 top right A portrait of the Duke of Alençon by François Clouet hanging in the drawing room. The work once belonged to Charles I as testified by the symbol on the back.

CULZEAN CASTLE

The windows look out onto the grey sea of the Firth of Clyde and the narrow strip of land called the Mull of Kintyre that ventures out into the ocean. Inside there is stucco-work, pastel colors and crystal chandeliers. It is in the salon of Culzean Castle on the Southwest Coast, a few miles from the celebrated Turnberry golf course, that the barren, romantic scenery of the region contrasts most magnificently with the elegance of the Georgian architecture and decoration of Robert Adam. The castle stands at the top of a cliff that drops sheer to the sea and is surrounded by the large estate inherited in 1744 by Sir Thomas Kennedy, the 9th Earl of Cassillis. The existing Medieval castle was composed of a round tower with a room on each floor, a purely defensive structure lacking any form of creature comfort. The Duke therefore decided in 1760 to add a long wing overlooking the sea. However, the new construction reflected his pragmatic spirit that was more interested in the modernization of the estate than in the elegance of his home. This situation changed seventeen years later when the Earl's brother David, the 10th Earl of Cassillis, called upon the most celebrated architect of the era, Robert Adam, to rebuild Culzean Castle and make it more suitable to the worldly lifestyle of the period.

66 top and center The traditional home of the Kennedy family; Culzean Castle, inherited by the 9th Earl of Cassillis in 1744, immediately took the place of Dunure, the family's ancient castle. Robert Adam's design has a classical linearity that, however, does not disdain Medieval touches such as the slits and crenellated turrets.

66 bottom Culzean Castle is surrounded by extensive grounds transformed into a Country Park, and a large walled garden, the lake of swans and various buildings such as Camellia House. A group of naturalist guides is at the service of visitors to provide guided botanical tours. The park headquarters was opened in 1970 in the Robert Adam-designed Home Farm.

66-67 and 67 top Set in a spectacular position at the top of a cliff dropping sheer to the Firth of Clyde, Culzean Castle dominates the whole of the West Coast, with views ranging over Arran and Kintyre. The imposing but severe exterior is softened by the large green lawns, the flower beds and the terraces on which even tropical trees flourish.

68 top left
The Saloon is probably the most beautiful room designed by Robert Adam. Every last detail has been taken into consideration, from the alternation of colors in the carpet, to the stucco-work of the chimney breast. What is most striking is the contrast and at the same time the continuity with the

wild natural environment of the West Coast that appears like a tromp l'oeil beyond the windows. Just a three hundred or so feet always is the cliff and the grey waters of the Firth of Clyde, while in the distance lies the Mull of Kintyre peninsula. The painting above the fireplace is by Deschamps.

68 bottom left
The damask wall coverings in the Drawing Room were woven especially for Culzean Castle by the Gainsborough Silk Weaving Company. The mirror set above

the fireplace is particularly fine and was made in 1976 to the designs of Robert Adam. It features the swans present in the coat of arms of the Cassillis family.

The old building was demolished and replaced with a round tower that accentuated the romantic aura of the complex as a whole. Inside, on the first floor, Adam designed the stunning Saloon, a symbol of the elegance of the century, and dealt personally with every last detail of the furnishing. The interiors in fact constitute one of the last and most successful works of the architect and his team of artists and craftsmen who had already proven their talents at the houses of

Hopetoun and Mellerstain near Edinburgh. The circular ceiling panels were painted by the Italian artist Antonio Zucchi, the marble fireplaces were the work of Peter Henderson of Edinburgh while the great round carpet was woven not far from Culzean to a specific design. Adam's masterpiece, though, is the oval staircase located in what was once a dark, cramped interior courtyard behind the tower. Sober and elegant, the staircase rises between two stories of Corinthian columns while the play of curved lines creates an impression of movement. When David Kennedy died in 1792 without heirs, Culzean Castle passed to his cousin, Captain Archibald Kennedy of New York whose home address was No. 1 Broadway. During the last century the symmetry of Adam's original design was lost with the construction of a new wing. In 1945, Charles Kennedy, the 14th Earl of Cassillis, presented the castle to the National Trust for Scotland on the condition that the upper floor was made available to General Eisenhower as a sign of the Scottish people's gratitude for his feats during the war. A great park extends around the castle in which woodland alternates with avenues of rhododendron and Italian gardens overlooking the sea. Artificial corridors link the fountain of the Court Garden to the large walled garden where the typically British art of contrasting flowers of various heights and colors is seen to best effect.

68 top right
The old dining room occupies the site on which the old castle once stood. It is currently furnished as a sitting room but its original function is revealed by the vine leaves and bunches of grapes around the fireplace. The three ceiling medallions were painted by Antonio Zucchi. Many of the furnishings such as the mirror above the fireplace, the urns over the doors, the candelabras and the draperies are identical to those designed by Adam.

68-69 Set adjacent to the entrance to the castle, the walls of the armory are decorated with compositions of swords and pistols from the West Lowland Fencible Regiment. The family coat of arms is surrounded by light dragoon pistols forming a large oval, while around the clock above the fireplace other pistols are set in a perfect circle.

69 top left The dining room occupies what were originally the library and the master dressing room. Vast and imposing, it is dominated by a long 18th-century table and Chippendale-style chairs. The painting above the mantelpiece by Ben Marshall dates from 1800 and depicts the 12th Duke of Cassillis, subsequently nominated Marquis of Aisla.

69 top, right The oval staircase is one of Adam's masterpieces and one of the principal features of Culzean Castle. It has a double row of Corinthian columns on the first floor and Ionic on the second to accentuate the perspective. The stairs, together with the banister and the red carpet, create a contrast of colors and curving lines.

DRUMLANRIG CASTLE

70 center left
The beautiful drawing room, richly decorated with wooden inlays, contains pieces of great value such as the two 17th-century French cabinets from Versailles, the magnificent portraits and the fine mirrors.

70 bottom left
Originally this attractive wood-paneled room was the entrance hall. Transformed into a dining room it has a stuccoed ceiling dating from the 19th century. Family pictures hang on the wall.

Drumlanrig Castle was originally built in the fourteenth century as a Douglas stronghold, but little trace of the early structure remains. The present castle with four corner towers was built by William Douglas, the 1st Duke of Queensberry in the decade between 1679 and 1691. It is the work of different architects, also Sir William Bruce is known to have worked on the plans, and the final result is a unique example of late seventeenth century Renaissance architecture in pink sandstone. When the castle was completed the Duke was so shocked by how much it had cost that he felt uneasy to live there. From an architectural point of view Drumlanrig constitutes the link between the fortresses built prior to the Act of Union and the "mock" castles constructed by the nobility as country houses. Drumlanrig has nothing of the Romantic fortified castles of other parts of Scotland. Its monumental appearance confers an air of great severity, unusual for a private home in the heart of the countryside. However, as soon as one enters the interior courtyard this austerity is mitigated. The entrance has a vaulted arch with Renaissance decoration and a Gothic structure supporting a terrace.

70 top left
The entrance hall is an attractive room lit by arched windows. Above the fireplace is exhibited a piece of embroidery said to have been done by Mary Stuart during her long imprisonment.

The large carpet on the floor with the coat of arms of the Douglas Heart family was woven in 1985. The hall's finest piece is the Rape of the Sabine Women attributed to Giovanni da Bologna (1524-1608).

70 right The oak staircase and balustrade were among the first of their kind Scotland. That which in all the other Scottish castles is a simple passageway, at Drumlanrig takes on the role of a veritable art gallery with paintings of international importance from the Madonna with Yarnwinder by Leonardo to the Old Woman Reading by Rembrandt along with other works by Hans Holbein, Murillo, Joost Van Cleef and a Madonna from the School of Correggio.

70-71 and 71 top Drumlanrig Castle, a pink sandstone construction, stands on a hill (Drum) and the end of a long (lang) ridge (rig). Surrounded by woods, this castle is one of the first examples in Scotland of the Renaissance style applied to civic architecture. Among the guests to have stayed at Drumlanrig were James VI, Bonnie Prince Charlie, Queen Elizabeth II and Prince Philip and also Neil Armstrong, the first man to have set foot on the moon.

72 top At Kirkwall, the capital of the Orkney Islands, off the North coast of Scotland, stand the beautiful ruins of Earl Patrick's castle, begun in 1607 by Earl Patrick Stuart, the brother of Mary Stuart and the illegitimate son of James V.

72-73 The dramatic ruins of Urquhart Castle stand on a promontory reaching out into Loch Ness. The castle, one of the largest in Scotland, fell into ruin after 1689. Most of what remains standing dates from the 16th century.

74-75 The walls of Eilean Donan Castle housed one of the great Scottish heroes, Robert the Bruce. Pursued by the English, the future King of Scotland was given refuge by John MacKenzie, the Lord of Kintail. Once crowned king, as a sign of his gratitude, Robert the Bruce sent a lieutenant to the castle, transforming it into one of the most important royal garrisons.

Inhabited ever since ancient times, as testified to by over 500 brochs, the defensive towers having been built 2,000 years ago, the Highlands has not always been an immense pasture for millions of sheep. Once upon a time the northernmost region of Scotland, this harsh, beautiful land, was covered with forests and the cultivated fields of the Highlanders, peoples of Celtic origin who lived in agricultural communities, the clans, ever ready to go to war at the behest of their chieftains. One of the most powerful of these clans was that of the McLeods; descendants of the Vikings of the Isle of Man. Their castle was at Dunvengan, on the Isle of Skye. The Scandinavian blood was mixed with that of the Celts of the Kingdom of Alba and reinforced the powerful clan communities which frequently engaged in struggles amongst themselves. The chieftains lived in defensive towers such as those of Eilean Donan Castle, the home of the MacKenzies, or Cawdor Castle, the residence of the Thanes of Cawdor. At the end of the Stuart dynasty the Highlands witnessed repeated revolts against the ruling house of Hanover. The region's castles such as Blair or Braemar changed ownership on a number of occasions and in some cases were transformed into barracks for troops. In 1715 there was an unsuccessful revolt led by the Duke of Mar who intended to bring James Edward, the younger son of James I, to the throne. The Highlanders were defeated at Sheriffmuir and the British army constructed new roads from Crieff to Fort William in order to keep the region under military control. Bonnie Prince Charlie returned from exile in France in 1745, landing in the Hebrides. He gathered all the clans faithful to the Stuarts at Glenfinnan and the following month entered Edinburgh, installing himself at Holyrood Palace. The rebel troops scored a victory at Prestonpans and advanced through the English Midlands as far as Derby. However, they were defeated at Culloden near Inverness in the April of 1746. Bonnie Prince Charlie had to flee and the repression of the Jacobites was ruthless. The survivors were forbidden to wear their kilts, to bear arms, to speak Gaelic and to play the bagpipes. The lands of the clan chieftains who had supported the Jacobites were confiscated and the clan system was dismantled. This marked the Highlanders' ruin. Accustomed for centuries to paying rent to the clan chieftain for their land in the form of military service, they were unable to find the money demanded by the new landowners. The English lords faithful to the Crown found it more convenient to transform their holdings into pasture or hunting estates. With the Highlands Clearances, the Highlanders were expelled from their lands, their houses were burned to prevent rebellions and any attempt at resistance was repressed. Many people emigrated and by 1860 the Highlands had been emptied. In the meantime, however, English society had developed a love of this wild and remote Scotland, so much so that Queen Victoria ordered the construction of Balmoral Castle, the royal family's current summer residence.

For centuries Dunrobin Castle has been the home of the Dukes of Sutherland, descendants of Freskin of Moravia who arrived in Scotland at the time of William the Lion. They immediately adopted the customs and culture of their new homeland, to the extent that they transformed themselves into Celtic chieftains and were invested in 1235 with the title of Earl of Sutherland. Their symbol, a Great Cat, led to the name Caithness, the northeastern region of the Highlands. Built on a terrace overlooking the sea, this castle with its turrets and pinnacles has no less than 187 rooms and is the largest home in northern Scotland. Dunrobin, whose name means the "Castle of Robin," is documented for the first time in 1401 as the fortress of the 6th Earl. However, there was also an older part, a Medieval tower dating from 1275, the remains of which can be seen in the windowed corridor. In the seventeenth century two wings were built to the south and the west to form an L-shaped plan. A wide tower with a circular plan united them to the Medieval fortress. In 1785 Elizabeth, the Countess of Sutherland, married Viscount Trentham, the Marquis of Stafford, an English noblemen and one of Europe's richest men thanks in part to the profits of the industrial revolution. A philanthropist with liberal ideas, he established large-scale programs for the improvement of the living conditions, the roads and the

76 top The elegant dining room was redesigned by Sir Robert Lorimer following the fire of 1915. The walls are fully paneled in wood and are topped with a classical frieze, probably of Italian origin. The room features a number of important family portraits. Above the fireplace Thomas Phillips has immortalized the sons of the 1st Duke; to the right is a portrait of Granville, the 1st Marquis of Stafford by George Romney and on the side wall, the Duchess Harriet, the wife of the 2nd Duke, with her eldest daughter, Elizabeth.

76 bottom This big silver cup occupies a first floor niche in one of the two turrets of Dunrobin Castle.

76-77 Overlooking the sea and surrounded by formal gardens of Franco-Scottish inspiration, Dunrobin Castle dates from the 13th century but was extended on more than one occasion from the 17th century onwards. The interiors feature furniture and paintings of great value as well as objects that recount the history of the family and Scotland itself.

77 top Seen from the terrace, the gardens of Dunrobin reveal the intricate design inspired by Versailles and the geometric pattern that develops around the fountain.

economy of the region. On the coast he had workers' houses constructed that he offered to the tenant farmers who unwillingly left their thatched cottages isolated in the Highland valleys. In reality he contributed to the depopulation of the Highlands. Over 5,000 families were evicted from the homes of their ancestors. Their place was taken by the sheep that are still today a constant feature of the region's landscape. During the last century almost the whole of the county of Sutherland in the Northwestern Highlands, that is to say, 1,300,000 acres of land, were owned by the Duchy, making it one of the greatest landowners of Western Europe. The current French-style castle owes its appearance to the 2nd Duke who in circa 1850 summoned Charles Barry, the architect of the House of Parliament in Westminster, in order to transform Dunrobin from a Scottish castle into a stately home. His wife, the Duchess Harriet, was a lady-in-waiting to Queen Victoria. The 3rd Duke constructed at his own expense the Highlands railway and the Victorian-style station that can still be seen not far from the castle. The castle itself features a library with a gigantic globe and hunting trophies and a Sicilian-style bedroom suite acquired by the Duke during a cruise through the Mediterranean. The castle is surrounded by a large park and an Italian garden with borders of roses and shrubs.

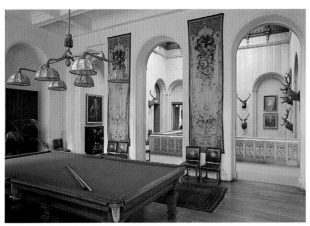

78-79 and 79
The new design for the drawing room, which was rebuilt after the fire of 1915, combined two smaller rooms so as to create a large airy salon with a beautiful view over the garden surrounding the great fountain. The ceilings, designed by Robert Lorimer, were created by Sam Wheeler in 1919. The furniture is from the Louis XV period, while the walls are covered with 18th-century tapestries depicting the life of the Greek philosopher Diogenes. The finest works are, however, the masterpieces by Canaletto hanging over the fireplaces.

79 top left The original billiards room designed by Lorimer is today used for the exposition of family heirlooms and ceremonial costumes. The billiards table has been placed in the Gallery, where hunting trophies can be seen behind the arches.

BRODIE CASTLE

Set in a 70-hectare park a few miles to the east of Nairn, for over eight centuries Brodie Castle was the home of the Brodie family. The castle dates from the fifteenth century with additions and extensions from the sixteenth, but it is thought that the original nucleus was first inhabited by the Brodies in 1160. All of the documentation relating to the origins of the castle and its rebuilding around 1560 was lost in the fire of 1645 when Lord Lewis Gordon, representing the Duke of Montrose, torched the castle during the civil war against the Covenanters. The castle was rebuilt and took on its present appearance in the seventeenth and eighteenth centuries. It features a Z-shaped plan with overhanging turrets and battlements. The extensions to the east, north and northeast made in 1824 are in the neo-Tudor style and were designed by William Burn. The oldest part of the building is the semi-basement kitchen in the North Wing. In 1982 ownership of the castle passed to the National Trust for Scotland.

CAWDOR CASTLE

*J*ust a few miles from Inverness and the Moray Firth, the Castle of Cawdor is associated with the Shakespearean tragedy, *Macbeth*. The tower with its entrance raised as a defensive measure, was built in 1380 by William Thane of Cawdor, a friend of King James II. Legend has it that a dream prompted him to allow a mule loaded with gold to roam freely and to build a castle at the very place where the animal stopped to sleep. The mule lay down beneath a hawthorn tree around which the original tower was constructed, arranged on four storys linked by a spiral staircase. In 1638 work began on the north wing and the old sitting room was linked by a stone staircase.

82 top left and 82-83 The gardens surrounding Cawdor Castle have a very intimate atmosphere. They are at their best from spring to late summer. The recently restored walled garden offers attractive combinations of colors.

82 bottom left and 83 top The severe, massive Cawdor Castle was built on a slight rise as the private fortress of the Thanes of Cawdor. In spite of the additions made over the centuries, it still has the appearance of a tower house with corner turrets and battlements.

82 right The family coat of arms is set into the walls of the castle that William Shakespeare used as the setting for the tragedy Macbeth *with the assassination of Duncan.*

84 top In spite of its bleak external appearance, Cawdor Castle has a surprisingly comfortable internal atmosphere. This is not so surprising when you consider that the castle is still the family home. Not all of the rooms are open to the public; the private areas include the intimate and welcoming dining and drawing rooms seen here.

84-85 The drawing room occupies what was once the old hall. The last major rebuilding work dates from the 16th century when a fireplace with the coat of arms of the Calders, the old form of Cawdor was added. Portraits of members of the family such as Pryse Campbell, the 18th Thane of Cawdor, dressed in an assortment of tartans, hang on the walls.

During the civil war the castle escaped lightly with only a few haylofts being torched by the royalist troops led by Lord Montrose. During Cromwell's bloody campaigns Cawdor Castle was allowed not to have to house soldiers and officers, thus safeguarding its rich interior furnishings. In 1684 the castle was transformed into a comfortable home by Sir Hugh Campbell, the 15th Thane. The windows were enlarged, carved fireplaces were installed and two new wings to house the Thane's nine children and numerous servants were built. Further improvements were made around 1720 and the middle of the nineteenth century, but without leading to significant modifications.

85 top The dining room features a late-Victorian style decorated ceiling and tapestries with scenes from the life of Don Quixote on the walls.

895 bottom The stairs are covered with a carpet that features the greens and blue of the Campbell of Cawdor tartan. Antique firearms are arranged decoratively on the walls.

BRAEMAR CASTLE

Braemar is a small village in the upper valley of the River Dee, famous throughout the world for the Royal Highlands Gathering, the traditional Highland games held each summer in the presence of the royal family.

Standing against the magnificent backdrop of the peaks of the Cairngorms the castle has a severe aspect, animated only by the play of turrets and battlements. It was built in 1628 by John Erskine, the Earl of Mar and the treasurer to King James VI. The fortress served as a lodge during hunting trips organized in the Grampian mountains, but also as a bulwark against the increasing power of the Farquharsons. In 1689, during the brief Jacobite rebellion, the castle was conquered and burned by the "Black Colonel," John Farquharson of Inverary, and for sixty years remained a ruined shell. The 39th Earl of Mar inspired the Jacobite rebellion of 1715, on the 6th of September of that year brought together the rebel troops at Braemar, where today stands the Invercauld Arms Hotel. At that time the castle was but a blackened skeleton and was requisitioned by the loyalist troops following the defeat of Mar and the Jacobites at Sheriffmuir. The castle was restored in 1748 and transformed into a garrison for the troops of the Hanoverian government. The very young Adam brothers, John and Robert, had a hand in

the reconstruction and went on, of course, to become extremely famous architects. The crenellated curtain wall dates from this period and was based on a star-shaped plan in accordance with Renaissance theories on fortifications.

At the end of the century the castle was converted back into a residence and housed Queen Victoria when she came to attend the Highland Games prior to the acquisition of Balmoral.

BLAIR CASTLE

Set in the heart of the wild Grampian mountains, at the foot of wooded slopes, Blair Castle has always controlled the main road between Edinburgh and Inverness. Its history is closely linked to that of Scotland itself and the struggles between the Highland clans.

The residence of the Dukes of Atholl ever since the time of the Celts, the castle was actually built in 1269 by

John Cumming of Badenoch who took advantage of the absence of the Earl, David, who was involved in the crusades. Hidden amidst the turrets and battlements there is the original tower, still known today as the Cumming Tower.

Over the centuries the castle was subjected to diverse modifications and additions. It also changed hands on a number of occasions due to a lack of heirs or political maneuvering. In 1457 the deeds to the estate were given by James I to his blood brother Sir John Stewart of Balvenie, the founder of the current dynasty and whose motto, conferred by King James III together with the order to put down the insurrection of the MacDonalds in the islands, was "Furth Fortune and fill the Fetters."

The male line was extinguished in 1625 and the title to the castle passed to John Murray, Lord of Tullibardine and a descendant on the maternal side. After his death, Blair Castle was occupied by the Duke of Montrose and in 1652 by Cromwell's troops. Claverhouse, the leader of the Jacobite rebellion, occupied the castle in 1689 and on the 27th of July of that year recorded a famous victory over the government troops in the narrow gorge of the River Garry near Killiecrankie.

The extension and rebuilding of the castle undertaken by the 2nd Duke was interrupted by the Jacobite revolt of 1745 when the pretender to

88 top The tapestry room on the second floor of Cumming Tower owes its name to the sumptuous tapestries woven in Brussels for Charles I.

88 bottom On the staircase, below a richly stuccoed ceiling, hang portraits of members of the family: the 1st Duke, John, immortalized by Thomas Murray, the 1st Marquis of Atholl, John, depicted by Jacob De Witt in the guise of Julius Caesar, and his wife, Lady Amelia Stanley.

88-89 When Queen Victoria visited Blair Castle in 1844 she described it as a "broad and simple white building." Twenty-five years later the 7th Duke commissioned John and David Bryce to rebuild the castle in the Scottish Baronial style we see today.

89 top The white structure of Blair Castle with its crenellated towers and conical roofs stands out against the green mountains of the central Highlands. Around the castle extends a large estate with sheep pastures, woods, gardens and cultivated land.

90 top The drawing room is the most beautiful room in Blair Castle, with walls covered with crimson damask silk and a ceiling decorated with elaborate stucco-work. Above the white marble fireplace hangs a family portrait by Johann Zoffany depicting the 3rd Duke, his wife and their seven children.

90-91 The Ballroom was built between 1876 and 1877 by the 7th Duke. Beneath a wooden ceiling with exposed beams, this room was used for balls, concerts, receptions and the world bagpipe championships. The partially paneled walls are decorated with various family portraits and hunting trophies.

the throne, Bonnie Prince Charlie, marched south with his army of Highlanders, staying for some days at Blair Castle. After being occupied by the troops of the reigning Hanoverian dynasty, in 1746 the castle was besieged by Lord George Murray, the 2nd Duke, at the head of his Atholl Highlanders. This was the last castle in Great Britain ever to be besieged and ironically enough it was by the owner himself. Once the situation had been resolved the 2nd Duke revived his modernization work, following the dominant Georgian style. In 1756 the portrait staircase on the walls of which the Lords of Atholl are immortalized was added. The last intervention dates from the late nineteenth century when between 1869 and 1904, the castle was restored in a Romantic vein. Today it is a white turreted manor house surrounded by an immense forest and pastures with hundreds of sheep.

The last Duke of Atholl, the 10th, who died in 1996 was also the only man in the entire United Kingdom with the right to maintain a private army, the Atholl Highlanders. On his death, the castle and the 70,000-acre estate was inherited by a charitable institute. The title on the other hand went to a distant South African cousin.

BALMORAL CASTLE

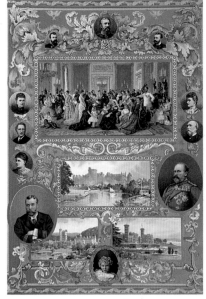

92 top left A vast estate of 20,000 hectares extends around Balmoral and ranges from the fertile lands of the valley to the heather-covered hills of the Lochnagar range dominating the area.

92 bottom left The tower stands out from the western facade, rising from the main body of the building, and at the top, below the arrow slits, can be seen a large clock.

Balmoral Castle, the summer residence of the royal family, stands in the upper Dee valley, not far from Braemar. Set at the foot of wooded hills, the castle is surrounded by a vast estate acquired in 1848 by Prince Albert and Queen Victoria, who had both fallen in love with the Highlands. When the royal couple visited Balmoral for the first time Queen Victoria described it in her diary as "a pretty little castle in the Scottish style, surrounded by wooded hills that recall Turingia, the birthplace of Prince Albert."
The castle was actually two hundred years old but had been rebuilt a few years earlier by the previous owner, Sir Robert Gordon. The building was not large enough for the needs of the royal family, for their numerous servants and for their state obligations.
In 1852 work thus began on the construction of a new castle in the Gothic Revival style to the designs of the architect William Smith.
The new residence in white granite was completed over the following years, while the royal family spent the summers in the old castle. Balmoral is composed of a massive square tower, embellished with four lateral towers and a long three-story wing with large panoramic windows that led Queen Victoria to write, "Not only is the house attractive and comfortable but it has a beautiful view, that the old castle did not."

92 top right The west wing of the palace overlooks the magnificent and painstakingly groomed Rose Garden with the statue of a chamois and the fountain. The luxuriant gardens are at their best when the royal family is in residence at Balmoral during the summer.

92 bottom right A family portrait with Queen Victoria at Windsor Castle in 1890 and views of the Balmoral and Sandringham. The images were reproduced in the volume published on the occasion of the sovereign's jubilee.

93 This aerial view reveals the layout of Balmoral Castle as a whole. The present-day structure is the fruit of numerous modifications made over the years to adapt the summer residence to the needs of the royal family.

94 *The Ballroom, the walls of which feature a bas-relief by John Thomas, overlooks the granite steps built in 1857 that lead to the fertile banks of the River Dee.*

95 The Ballroom is
the only room of the
castle open to the
public. Family
portraits and objects
of royal provenance
are exhibited in the
great room
illuminated by tall
windows.

96 top *Dunvegan Castle is the only stately home in the Western Isles and is the house inhabited the longest by a single family in the whole of Scotland. Among the visitors to the castle were James V and Sir Walter Scott.*

DUNVEGAN CASTLE

*O*verlooking Loch Dunvegan on the northwest side of the Isle of Skye, this castle has always been the home of the MacLeods, the lords of the isles. Tradition has it that Leod was the youngest son of the last Viking king of the Isle of Man and the Hebrides. When King Alexander II defeated the Vikings in 1263 at Lairg, Leod possessed at least half of the Hebrides.

The land of the MacLeods is still extensive but is today restricted to part of the Isle of Skye, Dunvegan Castle and its surroundings up to the Cuillins which rise barren and steep 3,260 feet above sea level.

In the thirteenth century, during the period of the first clan chieftain, the castle was no more than a defensive wall protecting a low building with a thatched roof. Around 1340, Malcom, the third MacLeod chieftain, added a massive square tower at the northeast corner of the house.

At the southeast corner there is an elegant fairy-tale tower built at the behest of Alasdair, the 8th chieftain, in around 1500. The tower's four floors are linked by a spiral staircase.

The present Romantic appearance dates from the Victorian era when the castle was extended between 1840 and 1850 by the 25th clan chieftain, to the designs of the architect Robert Brown of Edinburgh. The work cost the notable sum of 11,250 $.

96-97 and 97 top
All around Dunvegan Castle extends a large park crossed by footpaths that lead to two spectacular waterfalls. The benign influence of the Gulf Stream allows plants typical of lower latitudes such as rhododendrons and azaleas to flourish. A short distance away, on the sea shore, colonies of seals bask in the warmth of the sun.

97 bottom
For seven centuries the castle has belonged to the MacLeods and is associated with the legend of The Fairy Flag, a mysterious and extremely old silk banner of Middle Eastern origin which is said to have the magical ability to rescue the clan from peril. It is said to have been presented to a member of the MacLeod clan by an enamored fairy.

98 top
The spectacular ruins of the Marischals' impregnable fortress, Dunnottar Castle, stand on a cliff falling sheer to the North Sea near Aberdeen. The castle put up stubborn resistance to Cromwell's besieging troops.

CENTRAL AND EASTERN SCOTLAND

98-99 Over 400 years of history are enclosed within the powerful walls of Castle Fraser. Built in 1575 near Aberdeen by Michael Fraser, the 6th Lord, the two low wings help to emphasize the attractive central tower, making it one of the most beautiful castles in Scotland.

99 Built in sandstone, Kellie Castle in Fife dates from the 14th century. In 1573 a second tower was added to the east and the castle was completed between 1573 and 1605. The southeast tower, with the entrance portal, is a minor masterpiece with overhangs and corner turrets. The gardens are extremely attractive.

Undulating countryside that gives way to wooded hills, bucolic valleys that gradually transform in heather-covered moors: that central and eastern Scotland is a rich and fertile region is demonstrated by the dozens of castles constructed along the course of the River Dee or on Tayside, with a concentration greater than in any other part of the country, with the possible exception of the area around Edinburgh. This is the region of the royal castles of Stirling and Falkland and those of the manors tied to the crown such as Drummond and Glamis. But above all, it is the area in which the Scottish Baronial style of architecture with its towers, battlements and overhangs on a generally simple and linear base can be seen to best effect in buildings such as Craigievar Castle, Castle Fraser and Fyvie Castle.

Numerous stone circles show that these hospitable lands have been inhabited since prehistoric times. The earliest settlers were the Picts who lived here long before the Celts reached Scotland. The Roman legions arrived between the 1st and the 2nd centuries, established their base near Mons Grapius close to the present-day Stonehaven and there defeated the Scottish tribes. They did not remain for long, however, preferring to withdraw south of the wall constructed by Antoninus between the Clyde and the Firth of Forth.

In the 9th century Kenneth MacAlpine united the kingdom of Dalriada with that of the Picts, thus gaining control of much of Scotland. The capital of the new kingdom stood not far from Scone Palace, built with the stones of the ancient abbey. The thirteenth century saw power pass into the hands of the Comyns, the Counts of Buchan, following the marriage between a Comyn and the daughter of a local chieftain. Robert the Bruce's fight against the English was also a struggle against the Comyns, their allies. Then came the turn of the Gordons who exercised almost regal control over the northeast until 1562. This was the century in which the simple Medieval tower houses began to be transformed into vertical palaces. A typical example is Crathes Castle in the Dee valley, built towards the end of the sixteenth century. From the same period, and at a short distance away, is Castle Fraser which features decorative elements of French origin. Haddo House, designed by William Adam for one of the branches of the powerful Gordon family, was built in the Neoclassical and Georgian styles.

FYVIE CASTLE

100 top left and 101 top Fyvie Castle is surrounded by a great English-style park with ponds and lakes. The walled garden which features informal combinations of flowers of all colors is of immense appeal. The park is embellished with sculptures such as the statue of the dwarf of Queen Henrietta Maria, or the 16th-century urn sculpted from Venetian marble.

*F*yvie is a village set amidst the woods on the banks of the River Ythan, once famous for its freshwater pearls. Surrounded by a great park with a small lake, the castle is one of the best examples of Scottish Baronial architecture, with five towers commemorating the five great families to have owned the estate through the ages, the Prestons, the Meldrums, the Setons, the Gordons and the Forbes-Leiths.

Originally Fyvie was a royal fortress, surrounded by a hunting forest, as indicated by the Gaelic place name which means Hill of Deer. The castle occupied a strategic position: to the east it was protected by a great marsh and to the north and the west by the meanders of the river. The only line of attack was from the south where the single, well defended entrance led into an internal courtyard.

The oldest castle on the site was probably built in wood, with external defences in beaten earth. William the Lion visited Fyvie in 1211 (or 1214) and Alexander III conceded its statute to him. On the 31st of July, 1296, the English King Edward occupied Fyvie during his punitive campaign in Scotland. Some years later Robert the Bruce administered justice in the an open-air court in the castle's beech forests.

In the fourteenth century the castle took the form of a massive stone keep protected by a high curtain wall reinforced with corner turrets. The prin-

100 bottom left and 100-101 A jewel of Scottish architecture, Fyvie Castle emerges from the green countryside with towers and spires that are decoratively topped with statues of musicians. The castle is the fruit of repeated and successive modifications that fortunately have not compromised its harmonious architecture.

100 top right The coat of arms of the Forbes-Leith family, the last owners of the castle. In 1889, Alexander Leith, an American steel magnate, acquired the castle and embellished it with works of art.

cipal entrance through the south wall was defended by further towers, in all likelihood constructed during the period of Edward I's occupation.

The castle remained the property of the Crown until 1370 when it was presented by Robert II to his eldest son John, the future Robert III who in his turn presented it to his cousin, Sir James Lindsay, Lord of Crawford and Buchan. In 1390-91 Fyvie was reassigned to Sir Henry Preston, a cousin of Sir James, who took possession only in 1402. Having become the property of the Medurn family through marriage, Fyvie was sold in 1596 to Alexander Seton, the Chancellor of Scotland, who undertook major extension works and the creation of the triumphant ornamentation of the top floor and the roof that made of this castle a fairy-tale composition of overhanging turrets, decorated pediments, sculpted garrets and pinnacles in the form of hunters or musicians.

Support for the Jacobite cause led to the requisitioning of the Fyvie estate and, in 1694, Seton's grandson died penniless in a Parisian attic where he had fled after having backed the unsuccessful revolution of the Stuarts.

In 1733 Fyvie Castle was acquired by the 2nd Duke of Aberdeen for his third marriage and it was subsequently inherited by the first-born son of this union, William Gordon of Fyvie. At the end of the eighteenth century the new owner drained the

CHARTA ROBERTI III IN FAVOREM HENRICI DE PRESTOUNE MILITIS·

PRO REDEMPTIONE RADULPHI DE PERCY MILITIS ANGLICI ET PROSERVITIO SUO OMNIUM TERRARUM BARONIO DE FERNIARTIN INFRA VICECOMITATUM DE ABIRDENE

102-103 The entrance hall, furnished by William Gordon, replaced the old fortified entrance on the south side of the castle. The ceilings are richly decorated and the walls are covered with hunting trophies, arms and armor collected by Lord Leith. The armor came from Germany and dates back to the

16th-17th century. One can also admire a marble bust of Caesar Augustus and the perfectly preserved tusk of an elephant. The most impressive element of the furnishings is the fireplace, surmounted by a relief panel illustrating the Battle of Otterburn of 1388 in which Sir Henry Preston captured Ralph de Percy.

103 top left The dining room was furnished by William Gordon in 1790 and subsequently modified by Lord Leith. The red wall covering, the dark draperies and the stucco-work on the ceiling confer an austere and ceremonial atmosphere upon the room. There are numerous portraits hanging on the wall:

above the fireplace, in a carved wood frame, is the wife of Lord Leith, Marie Louise January; on the door to the servant's quarters hangs a portrait of Lord Leith himself while portraits of Sir William Maxwell of Calderwood and Sir John Stirling of Kippendarie with his daughter hang on the other walls.

103 bottom left A portrait of Ethel Louise Forbes-Leith painted by Luke Fildes in 1906 dominates the Back Morning Room. The sole heir of Alexander Leith, on the death of her father in 1925 she inherited the title that was eventually passed on to her son Andrew, born in 1929.

103 top right and bottom The Billiards Room is located at the base of the Gordon Tower, in what were until 1890 the kitchens. This room was the favorite of the male members of the family for games, smoking and drinking. The billiards table was made by Cox and Yeman of London. Various paintings with Scottish subjects hang on the walls: the most spectacular is The Sound of Many Waters *painted by Sir John Millais. Another depicts the Scots Greys at Waterloo, painted by Colonel F.S. Seccombe in 1891. Hunting trophies and arms are displayed above the fireplace. The castle also boasts an unusual room for bowling.*

marsh on the east side, created a lake, landscaped the park and added the Gordon Tower to the north of the West Wing. In 1885 his descendant, Sir Maurice Duff Gordon was obliged to sell the family estate to resolve his financial difficulties.

Four years later Fyvie Castle and its lands were acquired for 246,130 $ by Alexander Leith, a Scotsman born at Blackford, a few miles from the

castle, who had made a fortune in America, becoming one of the magnates of the steel industry. During his lifetime he embellished the castle with suits of armor, tapestries and paintings of the English and Scottish Schools. In 1890 he added the Leith Tower to the west of the Gordon Tower. In 1983, Sir Andrew Forbes-Leith put the property up for sale and after long negotiations it was sold to the National Trust for Scotland.

104 top left The portrait of William Gordon of Fyvie by the Italian Pompeo Batoni is one of the most interesting works of the 18th century. Painted in 1766, it differs from other portraits by the artist who generally lent a gentle air to his aristocratic sitters. Sir William instead wanted to be portrayed as a proud Scotsman in the family tartan, standing in front of the Coliseum as a reference to the heroes of the Roman empire. This portrait is one of the most valuable works preserved at Fyvie Castle.

104 top right and 104-105 The atmosphere of the Music Room which leads off the drawing rooms is typical of the Edwardian style of many British homes of the early 20th century; a blend of antique and modern. The walls are covered with 17th-century tapestries from Brussels woven to the original designs of Peter Paul Rubens. The French Renaissance is well represented by the marble fireplace dating from 1521 featuring extremely colorful tiles with oriental motifs that can clearly be seen in the detail. The organ and the tiffany lamp complete the precious furnishings of this room.

105 top This drawing room on the second floor of the Gordon Tower was built in 1790 as the Morning Room by General William Gordon and was subsequently modified. On the ceiling the stucco-work represents the family coat of arms. With its dark red draperies, the room reflects the tastes of the 18th century. The imposing portrait of General William Gordon painted by Pompeo Batoni is from this era. Above the mantlepiece hangs a portrait of Susanna Archer, the Countess of Oxford, by Sir Thomas Lawrence. Other valuable paintings bear the signatures of Gainsborough, Reynolds and Romney. The furnishing is prevalently Victorian or Edwardian, while the cabinets are in the Louis XV style.

105 bottom The small library contains a rich collection of books dealing with Scottish history and literature and topographical maps. This room was used by Lord Leith as a study. On his desk two electric bells kept him in contact with his assistants. Nautical decoration on the ceiling recalls Lord Leith's own naval career and his father's past as an admiral. Above the door hangs a copy of the portrait of William Elphinstone.

106 top left
This portrait of Lord Haddo was painted by Pompeo Batoni, an Italian exponent of the early neoclassical style.

106 top right
Haddo House was designed in 1731 by William Adam for the 2nd Earl of Aberdeen. Many of the splendid interiors date from the end of 19th century.

HADDO HOUSE

106-107 The library occupies the old stable block and is fully paneled in cedar wood inlaid with ebony. The rare books reflect the 4th Earl's interest in Greek and Latin texts and travel writing. All of the furnishings and the decor date back to the 19th century. Above the fireplace hang portraits of the 7th Earl and his wife Ishbel.

107 left The Morning Room occupies what in Adam's original design were three bedrooms. Transformed into a library by the 4th Earl, the space was eventually transformed into an informal sitting room. The fireplace, the mirror and the stucco-work date from the end of the 19th century. Note, between the two windows, the Irish satinwood cabinet given to the 7th Earl by his wife to commemorate his mandate in Ireland.

When Haddo house was built in the eighteenth century by William Gordon, the 2nd Earl of Aberdeen, to the designs of William Adam, the most famous Scottish architect of the day, it astonished the local nobility accustomed to living in romantic but hardly comfortable turreted castles. The great Palladian house with its two circular corridors linking the lateral wings contrasted with the barren surroundings of eastern Scotland. The construction of Haddo House was extremely expensive, partly because the finest materials were used. These included Norwegian timber for the roof which was completed in 1734 while the second wing was finished a year later. The ambitious Earl was not short of money, however, and he was known as a hard, inflexible land owner who exploited his tenants to the full. The 2nd Earl of Aberdeen died in 1745 and left the house to his son George, the 3rd Earl, a son from his first marriage (the heirs from the 3rd marriage instead received Fyvie Castle), but his amorous relations and worldly lifestyle left him with little time to devote to

property. It was George's grandson George Gordon, the 4th Earl, orphaned at 12 years of age and educated at Cambridge, who took Haddo House in hand. His interest in the Italian Renaissance led him to Italy, Greece, Turkey, Albania, Austria and Germany and resulted in him becoming known as the Athenian of Aberdeen. George Gordon took up a political career and between 1828 and 1830 was the Secretary of State for Foreign Affairs and between 1834 and 1835 the Secretary of State for the colonies. In 1852 he was entrusted by Queen Victoria with the task of forming a new government. Early in this century the 4th Earl commissioned the architect Archibald Simpson to extend Haddo House. William Adam's circular corridors were demolished and the lateral wings were extended: the North Wing contained the stables while the South Wing was reserved for the kitchens and the servants' quarters. Gordon summoned James Giles, a painter and garden designer, for the landscaping of the grounds. The last extension of Haddo House was made at the behest of the 7th Earl who, in 1877, revised the lateral elements in order to create new chambers for the family. In 1880 the architects Wardrop and Reid of Edinburgh definitively transformed the house to make it more suitable to the changing demands of the family. The new arrangement of the entrance and the staircase robbed the western facade of the purity of William Adam's neo-classical design.

107 top right The dining room has been preserved with its 1880 furnishings intact. Portraits of the family and of the Stuarts hang on the walls. The attractive table is laid with silver, crystal and porcelain.

107 bottom right Redecorated at the end of the 19th century, the drawing room at Haddo House is dominated by the painting of David and Goliath by Domenichino that hangs above the fireplace. Among the other pictures exhibited are a Head of St. Peter by Van Dyck and a portrait of Sir Walter Scott and his daughter by Sir William Allan.

CRAIGIEVAR CASTLE

Set in a secluded position in the picturesque Grampian Hills, Craigievar Castle is universally recognized as the best example of a tower house built in Scotland, a happy marriage of local tradition and exotic influences of French origin. Three storys rise on an L-shaped plan, with four in the central tower. In reality the castle is a house built vertically rather than horizontally, with spiral staircases taking the place of corridors. While the lower section is simple and austere, the upper floors are a play of projections, turrets, parapets and spires.

The first reference to Craigievar is found in a statute of 1457 conserved in the castle itself, which indicates the owners of the castle as the Mortimer family. The Mortimers began the construction of the castle, but late in the sixteenth century they suffered financial problems and were obliged to stop work and sell the property. The new lord of Craigievar Castle was William Forbes, the brother of the Archbishop of Aberdeen and a merchant who had made a fortune trading with the Baltic ports, earning himself the nickname Danzig Willie. The profits from his commercial enterprises refinanced the construction of the castle, leaving great expressive freedom to the master mason. Since then the descendants of the merchant have lived for centuries in the castle. In 1963 the property was donated to the National Trust for Scotland, a body that manages dozens of places of historical interest.

110 top left The Long Gallery takes up the whole length of one wing of the castle and is famous for its vaulted ceiling decorated with oak panels, one of the few in Scotland, with the exception of those of the royal palaces. In this century it was transformed into a library.

110 top right The name "Muse's Room" derives from the lively decoration of the ceiling depicting the Nine Muses and Seven Virtues. The female figures have led to a suggestion that the room was originally a ladies' drawing room. There is a particularly attractive tapestry designed by William Morris and made late in the 19th century.

CRATHES CASTLE

110-111 and 111 right The gardens at Crathes Castle are divided into eight thematic zones, set on two different levels and separated by yew hedges. They have been designed so that plants are flowering all year round.
The layout can be clearly seen in this aerial photograph.

111 left
A gardener intent on transforming a yew shrub into a sculpture.
The gardens are tended by four gardeners supervised by a head gardener. Much of the current layout was designed by Sir James Burnett and his wife, Lady Sybil, both green-thumbed enthusiasts.

Along with Craigievar, Crathes Castle is one of the best examples of Scottish architecture. Begun in 1553 by Alexander Burnett, it took over forty years to complete the fortress with its L-shaped plan, and it was finished thanks to his great-grandson. In 1656 it was inhabited by Burnett's grandson, the 12th Lord. The history of the building is commemorated in two shields on the eastern facade. The first contains the coat of arms of Alexander Burnett and Janet Hamilton with the date on which work began, the second contains those of Alexander Burnett (the great-grandson) and Katherine Gordon and the date it was completed.

Like all the castles in the Scottish baronial style, Crathes develops vertically. The upper part is a triumph of turrets, overhangs, pinnacles and false battlements while the lower section is more austere, in spite of the opening of Victorian-style windows on the first floor. During the last century an incongruous late-Victorian wing overlooking the upper garden was added. Destroyed in a fire in 1966, it is today restored, but the Victorian additions were not rebuilt. The magnificent eighteenth century grounds feature one of the richest collections of trees in the whole of Great Britain.

GLAMIS CASTLE

Glamis Castle, the home of the 18th Earl of Strathmore and Kinghorne, is one of the most famous castles in Scotland and the birthplace of Princess Margaret. A grandiose avenue leads to a fortified manor house in pink sandstone, all turrets and pinnacles, the result of the romantic additions of the nineteenth century.

Originally the castle was one of the many hunting lodges of the kings of Scotland, although the site had already been inhabited in earlier times. Around the eighth century St. Fergus had built a church there of which a sacred wall remains.

In 1372 Sir John Lyon received the Glamis estate as a gift from King Robert II and four years later he married the King's daughter Joanna. The castle of the epoch is incorporated in the present building, the ramified structure of which is the result of successive extensions. Originally the castle took the form of a tall, slim tower that was easily defended but provided inconvenient living accommodation. The ground floor was occupied by storerooms while the principal hall was located on the first floor and was reached via an external staircase.

In spite of the Lyon family's ties of kinship and centuries of fidelity to the Crown, in the sixteenth century it was deprived of royal support. The cause of the family's disgrace was the marriage between John, sixteenth Lord of Glamis, and a Douglas, the sister of the Earl of Angus, who was suspected of treason.

112 top and 113 top right On the lawn in front of the entrance to the castle stands a baroque sundial with diverse faces, decorated with rampant lions. Together with the turrets and the statues of James VI and his son Charles I, they are all that remain of the walls that once surrounded the castle.

*112 bottom
The detail shot of a roof shows the sculptural decoration at the summit of Glamis.*

112-113 This aerial view of the castle highlights the intricate design of the upper section, a feature of all the Scottish Baronial castles: the conical roofs of the towers and turrets, the battlements and the chimneys.

113 top left This plaque on the facade depicts the coat of arms of the Earl of Strathmore and Kinghorne: a lion and a horse rampant support a shield surmounted by a cross and closed with the motto "In te domine speravi."

114 top left The whole wing housing the dining room was demolished and rebuilt between 1775 and 1801. In 1851-53 the son of the 8th Duke of Strathmore designed this room with its unusual ceiling with pendant decorations, an impressive fireplace and oak paneling bearing the coat of arms of the 12th Duke of Strathmore.

114 bottom left This room occupies, in all probability, the former bedroom of the primitive hunting lodge. Its name, King Malcom's Room, is purely commemorative. The stucco-work decorating the ceiling is particularly fine.

114 bottom right The Queen Mother's Sitting Room is part of the royal apartments created by the Countess of Strathmore following the marriage of her daughter to the future George VI in 1923. The atmosphere is welcoming with tapestries, carpets and pink curtains. The dark, carved oak fireplace contrasts with the precious Chinese and Dutch porcelain exhibited on its shelves.

115 The pale pink color scheme of the drawing room enhances the gilded frames of the portraits on the walls. The ceiling is decorated with fine stucco-work featuring heraldic motifs. Among the paintings, the one by Auchterhouse portraying the 3rd Duke of Strathmore with his sons John, Charles and Patrick Lyon is worthy of particular mention.

Following the death of her husband, Lady Glamis was accused of witchcraft, imprisoned until she became blind and then burned alive in the square in front of Edinburgh Castle. Her young son was also imprisoned and the family property was requisitioned by the Crown. Thus between 1537 and 1542, James V, the future father of Mary Stuart, held court at Glamis with many royal edicts emanating from the castle. On the sovereign's death, John, the 7th Lord of Glamis, was liberated and, thanks to an Act of Parliament, regained his property. The furniture and silver had, however, disappeared following the passage to the royal court. John, the 8th Lord and the Chancellor of Scotland, restored the castle to its former glories. According to one of his guests, an English ambassador, the staff consisted of a butler, two manservants, a musician, a chief cook, a cellar master, a master mason, a head porter with his assistants, a bailiff and an officer. The lady of the house was attended by two ladies in waiting, a seamstress, a personal chambermaid and two further servants.

John's son Patrick was made Earl of Kinghorne by James VI whom he followed to London when, on the death of Elizabeth, the king of Scotland also became James I King of England. Patrick began to make a series of improvements to the castle which resulted in its present appearance, but misfortune was once again to strike at the doors of Glamis. John ran up

114 top right The lion rampant in brass in the dining room is one of the symbols of the Bowes-Lyon family. It was a present on the occasion of the 13th Earl's golden wedding anniversary in 1903.

114 center right The billiards room, built between 1773 and 1776, has a relaxing atmosphere, the walls

being lined with antique books and precious tapestries made in the 17th century. The stucco-work on the ceiling dates from 1903 and commemorates the 13th Earl's golden wedding anniversary. The large fireplace decorated with coats of arms came from Gibside, a property belonging to the Bowes family in the county of Durham.

huge debts in his support of the cause of the Covenanters who fought against the Church and the episcopacy. His successor Patrick, the 3rd Earl, thus found himself saddled with the astronomical debt of \$56,260. In 1670 he arrived at Glamis with his wife and began working to redress the situation. As soon as his financial circumstances began to improve he began work on the castle and was responsible for the transformation of the Great Hall into the Drawing

Room with elegant stucco-work on the vaulted ceiling and the decoration of the Chapel with painted wooden panels featuring biblical scenes. Tradition has it that in the left-hand corner at the back sits the ghost of the Lady in Grey, an unfortunate woman who died as the result of a tragic love story.

116-117 *The crypt has conserved its Medieval appearance. The walls are so thick as to be able to house a secret chamber in which legend has it that one of the Lords of Glamis and the Earl of Crawford, played cards with the devil. The furnishings in heavy oak combine well with the hunting trophies, arms and armor.*

117 top left *A copy of the beautiful portrait of the Queen Mother painted by De Lazlo when she was the Duchess of York hangs in her room. The recently restored four-poster bed has a frame of gilded and carved wood. The names of the 14th Earl, his wife and his children are embroidered on the inside of the canopy.*

117 right *The chapel is the most beautiful room in the whole of the castle, with its walls and ceiling fully paneled in painted wood with sacred scenes, from the Last Supper to the Flight from Egypt, by the Dutch artist Jacob de Wet.*

The Lady in Grey is not, however the only ghost to haunt the castle, being accompanied by the enormous and bearded figure of Earl Beardie who played cards with the devil and lost.

The opulent interiors belong to diverse periods from the fourteenth through to the nineteenth century, and contain collections of furniture, porcelain, paintings and historical objects.

The royal apartments are crammed with objects including photographs that document the relationships and the lives of the members of the family. The village of Glamis itself is composed of houses built in 1793 by the Earl of Strathmore for his estate workers.

These long, single-story constructions contain a schoolroom, a kitchen and a room for spinning and weaving wool.

118 top
The Mansfield coat of
arms has two red lions
rampant supporting
a shield surmounted
by a cross. The family
ancestors were of
Flemish origin and
came to Scotland in
the 12th century.

118 bottom With the
arrival of autumn,
the Gothic Revival
austerity of the
facade of Scone
Palace is softened by
the warmly colored
leaves of the creepers
almost completely
covering it,
accentuating its
romantic appeal.

SCONE PALACE

Although the massive stone palace on the banks of the Tay outside Perth dates from the first half of the nineteenth century, Scone is one of the oldest and most sacred sites in the whole of Scotland. Within the estate, in fact, rises Moot Hill, a place name deriving from the Gaelic *Tom-a-mhoid,* meaning "a place where justice is administered." It was here in 846 that Kenneth MacAlpine founded Celtic Abertha, the capital of the unified kingdom of the Scots and Picts. From that date onwards the Scottish kings were crowned on the consecrated Stone of Destiny, brought by MacAlpine from Dunstaffnage. Even when Edward I of England carried the stone to Westminster Abbey in London, where it was incorporated into the Coronation Throne, the Scottish kings continued to be crowned at Scone. On the same site around 1120, King Alexander I founded the first Augustinian monastery in Scotland. The abbey and the abbot's palace were also used as a residence by the royal family. The monastery complex enjoyed great prosperity during the reign of Robert III and the rising city of Edinburgh was annexed to the abbey so that it could benefit from its great wealth. In 1210 William the Lion founded a royal settlement a short distance away, on the site of what is today the city of Perth. On the 27th of June, 1559, the monastery was sacked by the fanatical followers of John Knox, inflamed by one of his sermons held at St. John Street in Perth.

118-119 Scone
Palace is surrounded
by a lawn across
which pheasants
wander undisturbed.
In the wood there is a
plantation of exotic
conifers established in
1848. Among the
specimen trees are a
number of Douglas
firs which owe their
name to the botanist
David Douglas who
was born and worked
on the estate.

119 top left Rising
in front of Scone
Palace, The Moot
Hill has a small
church that, like the
palace, was rebuilt in
the Gothic style in
1804. A finely carved
alabaster monument
commemorates
David, the 1st
Viscount Stormont
who according to the
legend built a church
on this hill in 1624.

119 top right
The ancient entrance
to Scone Palace can
be seen in the
background, beyond
the great lawn.
Although partially
ruined, it still bears
the coats of arms of
James VI and the 1st
Viscount. A short
distance from the
entrance stands the
Mercat Cross.

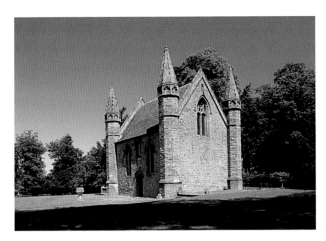

120 top The Ambassador's Room is dominated by the purple four-poster bed carrying the coat of arms of King George III and the royal monogram. The bed was presented to Lord Stormont when he was the ambassador to the French court. On the walls hang a portrait of him by Allan Ramsay and another

of Lady Elizabeth, the ambassador's daughter, with Dido the daughter of the chambermaid the Duke had freed from slavery.

120-121 The Long Gallery is in fact around 142 feet long, an unusual size for a Scottish house which were generally developed vertically.

The feet of many sovereigns have trodden the wooden floors inlaid with blackened peat bog oak. In 1580 the ceiling was frescoed with hunting scenes featuring James VI and his court, but was covered over at the beginning of the 19th century with a more sober Gothic-style ceiling.

121 top left The dining room is very airy and filled with one of the richest collections of ivory in Europe. The long table, covered with a damask cloth bearing the coat of arms of the Mansfields, is laid with a Chamberlain of Worcester tea service decorated with a profusion of fruit and flowers within a blue rim. The chairs are in the Chippendale style. Above the fireplace hangs The Philosopher *by Salomon Koninck and, on the right, a portrait of the 1st Earl of Mansfield.*

121 bottom left Overlooking green pastures, the old library now contains few books. They have in fact been replaced by examples of Meissen, Sèvres, Ludwigsburg, Chelsea, Derby and Worcester porcelain. These were pieces collected by the 1st and 2nd Earls for everyday use. Above the fireplace hangs the portrait of William Murray, the 1st Earl of Mansfield, by Martin.

121 right This spacious, North-facing drawing room has two fireplaces dating from the 17th century. Above them are two paintings by David Teniers, one depicting a group of dromedaries, the other a group of monkeys. There is also an impressive seven-feet tall brown bear killed by Sir Lancelot Carnegie when he was the British ambassador to Russia.

The ruins of the royal town and the monastery, and the great estate surrounding them, became the property of the Earls of Gowrie who in the sixteenth century constructed Gowrie Palace using the stones of the old abbey. Following the obscure Gowrie Conspiracy in which James IV would have been killed had he not been rescued by Sir David Murray, the property of the Gowries reverted to the Crown. As a reward the estate was presented to the Murray family, of noble Flemish ancestry and future Earls of Mansfield. Early in the eigteenth century, the 5th Viscount David opposed the Act of Union and during the revolt of 1715 gave hospitality to James III, the Old Pretender, at Scone Palace. His son the 6th Viscount, in his turn opened the doors of the palace to Bonnie Prince Charlie during the revolt of 1745. The viscount's brother William Murray became one of the greatest legal experts of the era and was invested as Earl of Mansfield. However, he lived in Bloomsbury, London, and was too busy to visit Scone. The 2nd Earl found the palace too damp and absolutely unsuitable for living in. It was not until the middle of the last century that the 3rd Earl commissioned the architect William Atkinson to construct a palace in the Neo-Gothic style, the building that can be admired today. Its massive external appearance with numerous lateral towers belies the wealth of the collections of French furniture, clock, tapestries, ceramics and ivory conserved inside.

DRUMMOND CASTLE

*122 left and 123
In spite of the
modifications made
during the last
century, Drummond
Castle still retains
all the features of a
17th-century Scottish
Renaissance castle.
It is located on a rise
with terraces
dropping away
towards the gardens.*

*122 right
The garden's design
changed throughout
the centuries. One of
the artificers of the
Renaissance
transformation
of the castle and the
garden was John
Drummond, the 2nd
Earl of Perth who
lived between 1584
and 1662.*

D rummond Castle stands on a rocky outcrop, two miles out of Crieff in the heart of Perthshire. Around 1490, Sir John Drummond of Stobhall was given permission by James IV to construct a fortress on land that he had acquired in the Strahearn Hills. James IV, a frequent visitor to Drummond Castle, fell in love with Sir John's daughter, Margaret, but the Scottish noblemen were determined that their sovereign should marry the sister of the English king, Henry VIII and therefore poisoned the young Margaret.

In 1605, on the orders of James VI, the 4th Lord Drummond traveled to Spain with the delegation entrusted with the task of negotiating a peace treaty between the two nations. This enterprise earned him the title of Earl of Perth. The new earl had a wing added to the original tower on the north side. His brother John, the 2nd Earl of Perth, a privy counselor to James VI and Charles I, transformed the castle by adding a low Renaissance-style element between 1630 and 1636, as recorded in the dates incised together with the family coat of arms. The architect of the extension was John Mylne who was also responsible for the sundial obelisk standing in the center of the garden. During the period of suppression by the English army under the leadership of Cromwell, the castle was badly damaged. In 1715 it became a garrison for the troops faithful to the crown and after 1745 the lands of the

Earls of Perth, including Drummond Castle, were confiscated as punishment for their support of the Jacobite cause. Formal gardens in the Renaissance style are laid out at the foot of the castle and are considered to be the most beautiful in Scotland. Box hedges and examples of topiary create a play of light and shadow on the emerald lawns and gravel paths, while the rose garden and the flower beds lend splashes of color to the composition.

124 top Italian influences can be seen in the gardens at Drummond in the form of the statues, the fountains and the urns adorning the balustrades. It is thought that many statues were bought in Italy by Charles Barry around 1830.

124 bottom In September 1842 Queen Victoria stayed at Drummond Castle for three days and recorded in her diary: "Sunday, 11th September... We walked in the garden and it is really very fine with terraces, like an old French garden." The following day, while Prince Albert was hunting in the forest of Glen Artney, the queen strolled amidst the flowers accompanied by the Duchess of Norfolk.

124-125 and 125 top From the upper terrace the garden appears in all its glory with the avenues and shrubs tracing the cross of St. Andrew with the 17th-century sundial at the center. Around the base, a mosaic of black and white pebbles forms the Drummond coat of arms.

128 Built around 1382 by Sir William Keith on the coast to the South of Aberdeen, the powerful fortress of Dunnottar Castle stands on a promontory overlooking the sea. Zeffirelli filmed Hamlet starring Mel Gibson here. Besieged by Cromwell's troops for eight months in 1654-2 Dunnottar became tragically famous for having been the harsh prison for over one hundred Covenanters who died here.

INDEX